Spelling Plus™

1000 Words toward Spelling Success

Susan C. Anthony

Nature's Workshop Plus, Inc.
P.O. Box 425
Danville, Indiana 46122-0425
www.workshopplus.com

Teach with less effort, more SUCCESS!

Susan Anthony's materials are designed to help teachers maintain high objective standards while helping *all* children reach them. Nurture the excitement of learning in your students, build their confidence with early success, and build a framework of background information to which new learning can be connected throughout life.

Susan's books are available from:
Nature's Workshop Plus
P.O. Box 425
Danville, IN 46122-0425
mail@workshopplus.com
www.workshopplus.com
Phone: (888) 393-5663
Fax: (866) 279-2505

Contact Susan at:
Susan C. Anthony
P.O. Box 111704
Anchorage, AK 99511-1704
Susan@SusanCAnthony.com
www.SusanCAnthony.com
Phone: (907) 345-6689

Books by Susan C. Anthony include:

Reference	*Facts Plus: An Almanac of Essential Information*
	Facts Plus Activity Book
	Encyclopedia Activity for use with The World Book Encyclopedia
Spelling	*Spelling Plus: 1000 Words toward Spelling Success*
	Dictation Resource Book for use with Spelling Plus
	Homophones Resource Book
	Spell Well: A One-Year Review for Older Students
	Personal Dictionary
Mathematics	*Addition Facts in Five Minutes a Day*
	Subtraction Facts in Five Minutes a Day
	Multiplication Facts in Five Minutes a Day
	Division Facts in Five Minutes a Day
	Casting Nines: A Quick Check for Math Computation

Note: Although the author and publisher have exhaustively researched all sources to ensure the accuracy of the information contained in this book, we assume no responsibility for errors, inaccuracies, omissions or any other inconsistency herein. Any slights against people or organizations are unintentional.

ISBN 1-879478-20-X

CONTENTS

TIPS FOR SURVEYING *SPELLING PLUS*

- Scan the Contents (p. iii) for an overview of *Spelling Plus*. If any section is of special interest to you, turn to it and read it in depth.

- Use the General Index (p. 164) to go straight to any specific information you want, such as how "invented spelling" is treated in this program.

- Read pp. v–vi for the key ideas underlying this program.

- Scan the article entitled "Why Can't My Child Spell?" on pp. 155–156 for a summary of the background information contained in this book.

- Scan pp. 26–28 for an overview of the components of *Spelling Plus*.

- Look at any reproducible spelling list (pp. 78–136). The ten blank spaces at the bottom allow for the flexibility of this program. They can be used for personal words, mixed review words, or in any way a teacher chooses. Use is optional.

- **Important:** Review starting with List 1 and begin group instruction with any appropriate list, regardless of the actual ages or grade levels of students. Words on early lists are *far* more important and common than those on later lists.

- See pp. 152–154 for a step-by-step checklist to guide you through the first several weeks of school as you introduce this program to students.

- You may wonder what to do after students have studied and mastered all 1000 words. Celebrate! You have options. *Spelling Plus* provides a method that can be used to teach *any* words students need to learn. Collect words misspelled in student writing, use words from subject area studies, or compile lists of challenge words. You may choose to discontinue the daily practice activity and use the time previously spent on it for creative writing or *anything* you want or need to teach. In any case, continue to dictate sentences and to teach and reinforce language skills with dictation. Continue weekly testing with review words to maintain mastery.

INTRODUCTION

As I taught 6th grade students the writing process, I found myself struggling with the problem of spelling. I was struck by the fact that many students who earned good grades on weekly tests did a poor job of spelling in their own writing. Not only did they misspell words from the previous week's list, they consistently misspelled basic and common words.

It was impossible for me to ignore spelling and mechanical deficiencies in student writing. I did not want to mark papers with a red pen, yet I felt uncomfortable allowing students to continue to practice errors without comment.

I took the problem as a challenge. It was my conviction that a truly effective spelling program would lead to improved spelling in first-draft writing, and that such a program need not require a disproportionate amount of teacher time and energy. I set out to find something that would *work* and be practical.

Spelling Plus is the result, and includes everything I found *most* valuable in improving student spelling while conserving my own time and energy. It is based on the following ideas:

- It is important for children to become successful spellers for these reasons:
  1. Judgments about a person's intelligence, literacy and the quality of his/her education are often based on competence in spelling.
  2. Good spelling is an important courtesy to the reader.
  3. Spelling is an indication of a person's attention to detail and quality.

- Formal spelling instruction should take as little time as needed to accomplish the goal of competency. Individualized spelling may be ideal, but it is impractical in most classrooms. *Spelling Plus* allows for efficient, effective use of time and energy.

- Spelling ability is largely a talent. Spelling is much easier for some people to learn than others. But nearly everyone, regardless of talent, can become a competent speller. Instruction should be to all learning modes and should be flexible enough to challenge gifted students while providing extensive review for children having difficulty.

- About 90% of text in English consists of just 1000 words. The most basic and frequently-used words should be memorized and overlearned, so that they can be spelled as easily and correctly as a child's own name. Once words have been *mastered,* they will be spelled correctly at all times, even in first-draft writing.

- Writing is the *purpose* for spelling, but spelling is best taught separately from creative writing using methods of direct instruction. Teachers then help students "bridge the gap" between spelling and writing. As students gradually master spelling, they will no longer need to devote much conscious thought to it. They will be able to write creatively *and* correctly.

- Spelling a word correctly on a weekly test is just the *first* step towards mastery. Most students will need extensive mixed review, dictation, and practice with editing before they will consistently spell well in their writing. Time must be provided for this.

- Teachers will be most successful when using methods that support their philosophies and preferences. Although effective methods are recommended in *Spelling Plus,* a schoolwide program will succeed if teachers at each level ensure that all of their students master 165 of the 1000 words using *any* methods. This is a *minimum* requirement. Teachers are free to supplement and expand the core program as suggested or as they choose.

Signs of a Successful Speller

All students are expected to become successful spellers according to these criteria:

- Acceptance of personal responsibility for correct spelling in one's own writing.
- Mastery of the most common and useful words and rules.
- A systematic and adequate method for approaching the study of new words.
- Independence in using the dictionary and other memory aids.
- Recognition of regular and irregular spellings (*state* v. *great*).
- An understanding of word construction, roots, prefixes and suffixes (*made* v. *played*).

Steps to Mastery of a Spelling Word

Spellings have not been *mastered* until they seem "easy" and are written correctly in first draft writing. The weekly test is just the *first* step. Without extensive mixed review and dictation, the time spent memorizing a weekly list may essentially be wasted. There are five steps toward mastery of a spelling word. The word is spelled correctly:

1. On the weekly test.
2. On a mixed review test.
3. In dictation.
4. In final draft writing. Mistakes in first draft writing are caught and corrected as the work is edited.
5. In first draft writing and at all times.

Recommended Teacher-Directed Daily Group Activities

Teachers may use any techniques they choose to teach the words. Two are recommended:

Daily Practice Activity with the weekly list of 15–20 words. This is a routine that takes 10–12 minutes per day. Students do the following steps orally under teacher direction. The homework routine is similar.

1. *Spell the word and read it.*
2. *Trace the word and read it.*
3. *Cover the model. Write the word and read it.*
4. *Check from the model.*
5. *Check and correct the word you wrote.*
6. *Close your eyes. Spell the word and say it.*

Daily Dictation of four sentences. This takes 15–20 minutes a day, depending on the amount of language-related instruction.

1. *The sentence is, "Who's coming?"*
2. *Say, "Who's coming?"*
3. *Students say the sentence.*
4. *Write, "Who's coming?"*
5. *Students write the sentence.*
6. *Teacher asks if there is anything special to remember about the sentence (apostrophe in contraction, question mark).*
7. *Teacher writes the sentence correctly.*
8. *Students check and correct their sentences.*

The Creative / Critical "Bridge"

Creative and critical thinking are incompatible and should not be taught at the same time using the same methods. Teach spelling separately from creative writing and help students "bridge the gap" with editing, dictation and personal words.

Editing — Personal Words — Dictation

Creative
The Writing Process
Brainstorming
Rough Draft
Sharing
Focus is on *Ideas*

Critical
Direct Instruction
Spelling
Punctuation
Capitalization
Focus is on *Form*

INCREDIBLE ENGLISH

Of some 5,000 languages in the world, less than half are written. Only 30 are spoken by more than a million people. Of these 30, English has the distinction of being more widely spoken than any language in history. It's the native tongue of some 400 million people and an important second language of 300 million more, many of them in Africa where it facilitates communication between members of various tribes. English is used in some way by at least one in seven people on the globe. Although Chinese has more speakers, it is rarely used by non-Chinese. In fact, there are currently more Chinese studying English than there are *people* in the United States.

English is an official language in more than 70 countries. It is used in:

> 50% of the world's books
> 60% of the world's radio programs
> 65% of scientific papers
> 70% of international mail
> 80% of computer text

English has the largest and richest vocabulary of any language, estimated to be between 600,000 and 2,000,000 words! And the vocabulary is growing. A report in the New York Times estimated the increase at 15,000 to 20,000 words a year!

Although we may not like it, it's a universal language, the most widespread—much easier to learn than Russian and more precise above all in technical matters.
—Fidel Castro, explaining why English was being added to the curriculum in Cuban schools

OUR QUEER LANGUAGE

When the English tongue we speak
*   Why is **break** not rhymed with **freak**?*
Will you tell me why it's true
*   We say **sew** but likewise **few**?*
And the maker of a verse
*   Cannot cap his **horse** with **worse**.*
***Beard** sounds not the same as **heard**;*
*   **Cord** is different from **word**.*
*Cow is **cow** but low is **low**,*
*   **Shoe** is never rhymed with **foe**.*
*Think of **hose** and **dose** and **lose**,*
*   And think of **goose** and not of **choose**.*
*Think of **comb** and **tomb** and **bomb**,*
*   **Doll** and **roll**, **home** and **some**.*
*And since **pay** is rhymed with **say**,*
*   Why not **paid** with **said**, I pray?*
*We have **blood** and **food** and **good**;*
*   **Mould** is not pronounced like **could**.*
*Wherefore **done** but **gone** and **lone**?*
*   Is there any reason known?*
And, in short, it seems to me
*   Sounds and letters disagree.*
*   —Evelyn Baring, Lord Cromer*
*   Spectator, Aug. 9, 1902*

*I take it you already know
Of **tough** and **bough** and **cough** and
 dough?
Others may stumble, but not you
On **hiccough**, **thorough**, **slough** and
 through.
Well done! And now you wish, perhaps,
To learn of less familiar traps?*

*Beware of **heard**, a dreadful word
That looks like **beard** and sounds like
 bird.
And **dead**, it's said like **bed**, not **bead**;
For goodness sake, don't call it **deed**!
Watch out for **meat** and **great** and **threat**,
(They rhyme with **suite** and **straight** and
 debt.)
A **moth** is not a moth in **mother**.
Nor **both** in **bother**, **broth** in **brother**.*

*And **here** is not a match for **there**,
And **dear** and **fear** for **bear** and **pear**,
And then there's **dose** and **rose** and
 lose,
Just look them up, and **goose** and
 choose,
And **cork** and **work** and **card** and **ward**,
And **font** and **front** and **word** and **sword**.
And **do** and **go**, then **thwart** and **cart**.
Come, come, I've hardly made a start!*

*A dreadful language? Why, man alive!
I'd learned to talk it when I was five.
And yet, to spell it, the more I've tried,
I hadn't learned at fifty-five.*

—T. S. Watt
The Manchester Guardian
June 21, 1954

ENGLISH SPELLING IS "TRUELY DIFICULT"

WHAT MAKES ENGLISH SPELLING HARD?

The Latin Alphabet Didn't Suit the English Language
— English was spoken long before it was written. The Latin alphabet had fewer letters than English had sounds.

Sounds Can Be Spelled in More Than One Way
— **Consonants.** English has 21 consonants, 24 consonant sounds, and some 115 different spellings for those sounds. The following words show some ways the hard **g** sound is spelled: *get, egg, **gh**ost, **gu**ide, ro**gu**e, mort**g**age.*
— **Vowels.** English has six letters which can represent vowels (**a, e, i, o, u,** and sometimes **y**). There are 15 vowel sounds and more than 107 ways to spell those sounds. The following words show some ways the $\bar{o}$ sound is spelled: *no, sew, rode, grow, loan, toe, oh, brooch, soul, though, beau, faux pas, yeoman, depot.*
— **Schwa sound** ("uh"). This most common sound in the English language may be spelled with almost any vowel or digraph in an unaccented syllable. Some examples include: *around, different, charity, contain, minimum, porpoise, pageant, certain, biscuit, Brooklyn.*

Letters Can Represent More Than One Sound
— **Consonants.** The letters **ch**, for example, are used to spell *church, charade,* and *ache.*
— **Vowels.** The letters **ea**, for example, are used in *break, pear, heart, threat, bead* and *earth.*
— **Combinations** such as **ough** confuse spellers. Consider the pronunciations of this combination in the following silly sentence: *He went through a rough day with a cough and a hiccough, though.*
— **Silent letters** plague spellers. In many cases, these were once pronounced, but spellings were never updated. For example: *thumb, indict, gnaw, honor, knife, salmon, hymn, island, listen, answer.* And of course, there are silent vowels: *bread, give, height, business, people, guide.*

Most "Rules" for Spelling Have Many Exceptions
— Although some rules are helpful, memorizing a large number of rules with their exceptions is probably more difficult than simply memorizing spellings. One rule that often holds is "**i** before **e** except after **c** or when sounded like **a** as in n**ei**ghbor and w**ei**gh." Yet consider some of the exceptions: *either, leisure, seize, weird.*

IS SPELLING DIFFICULT IN EVERY LANGUAGE?

No! Spelling Is Much *Easier* in Some Languages
— **Spanish** and **Italian** are spoken more crisply and distinctly than English and have an almost perfect sound-letter correspondence. Generally, there is one, and only one, letter for each sound and one sound for each letter. Once a student has learned the phonetic code, there is little need for spelling instruction.

Spelling Is Much *More Difficult* in Other Languages
— **French** is one of the most difficult Indo-European languages to spell. Final consonants are rarely pronounced. Inflected verbs sound the same but are spelled differently. Sounds have numerous spellings and there are four different accent marks!
— **Japanese** students must not only master two phonetic systems of writing, hiragana and katakana, they must also learn kanji, Chinese pictographs and ideographs which have passed into Japanese writing. Although the Japanese government has tried to reduce the number of Chinese characters to about 1,850 and simplify their shapes, learning to write correctly in Japanese takes years! In addition to the three systems of writing already mentioned, schools teach the Latin alphabet as well as three systems of Romanized Japanese! To further complicate matters, words have numerous meanings. The word *ka,* for example, has 214 separate meanings.
— **Chinese** students don't learn a phonetic code. Instead, they must commit to memory at least 4,000 of the 50,000 Chinese ideographs in order to be able to read (or write) a newspaper or modern novel. Chinese typewriters are enormous and even the best typists can manage only about ten words a minute. An advantage of Chinese is that, since the characters stand for ideas, they can be read by people who have such different dialects that they cannot understand each other's speech.

Take Heart, English Could Be Worse
— English does not have the many diacritical marks which writers of other languages must master such as accent marks and cedillas (ç). In Hungarian, *Szár* means "stem." *Szar* (without the accent mark) is a "bad word."
— All other major languages in the Indo-European family have grammatical gender. Nouns may be masculine or feminine. Learners of these languages must know each noun's gender in order to write (or speak) correctly.

It would not be easy to imagine a system of spelling more complex and inconsistent than that of English.
—M. M. Mathews
Words: How to Know Them

French
*In the following forms of **parler** (to speak), all but the fifth and sixth forms are pronounced identically:*

je parle	**nous parlons**
tu parles	**vous parlez**
il parle	**ils parlent**
elle parle	**elles parlent**

Japanese
Kanji: Chinese characters.

甘 开 至 臼 舟

Katakana: Square-shaped characters, used for emphasis.

シ ス セ ソ タ チ ッ

Hiragana: Rounded characters, used to spell words for which kanji has no characters.

あ い う え お か き

To this day in China, and other countries such as Japan where the writing system is also ideographic, there is no logical system for organizing documents. Filing systems often exist only in people's heads. If the secretary dies, the whole office can fall apart.
—Bill Bryson
The Mother Tongue

4

Our Spelling Is a Muess!

Although this comment may be tright,
Our English spelling is a fright!
We should develop some technique
That wouldn't make it quite so blique.
If only we could make some rules
That children, when they go to skules,
Could learn, and wouldn't have to guess,
We might see more effectivenuess.
The words would roll right off their tongue,
And they might learn to read quite
*   yongue.*
If we would spell with some technique,
They'd learn to read in just one wique!
Yet many people take to heart
The problems that such change would
*   steart.*
American printers from ocean to ocean
Would all protest with great commocean;
While changing, adjustments would have
*   to be made—*
Teachers would want to be doubly pade.
It might cause a great amount of trouble
To burst this awful spelling bouble.
How did our spelling get in this muess?
There are several reasons why, I guess.
Some borrowed words retained their signs
To show their etymological ligns.
The problem of spelling began to weigh
When words got easier to seigh
And spelling stayed the same as before
This caused a problem, or three or fore.
Printers, spelling's greatest friends,
Started several spelling triends.
Foreign printers printed words
With spellings that were "for the bords."
They changed the spelling of words like
*   ghost;*
They left some words, but altered mhost.
They added letters to save their rows,
Or subtracted some—this caused more
*   wows.*
Uneducated printers would

(continued on next page)

Our Words Are Doors to the Past

English is a patchwork quilt of languages!

450 A.D. to 500 A.D. — Anglo-Saxon Invasions
— The first "English" was spoken by **German**ic tribes that invaded the island of Great Britain. About 30% of modern English words are from Anglo-Saxon, including many with now-silent letters that were once pronounced. Some Anglo-Saxon words are *laugh, right, cow, school,* and *two.*

597 A.D. — St. Augustine Introduced Christianity
— **Latin** words were borrowed by the Anglo-Saxons both before and after they invaded Great Britain. Many of these had to do with the church. Some Latin words are: *priest, camp, candle, cheese, cup, mile, pound, street* and *wall.*
— Many **Greek** words came into the language through Latin. For example: *atom, chorus, phrase, music, poetry, pneumonia* and *rhubarb.* Although most European languages changed the **ph** to **f** in words borrowed from Greek, in English the original spellings were retained.

789 A.D. to 1040 A.D. — Danish Invasions
— During the Middle Ages, Great Britain was repeatedly attacked by Vikings. Words such as *birth, dirt, egg, fellow, guess* and *race* came from their language, **Old Norse.**

1066 A.D. — Norman Conquest
— The Normans defeated the English in 1066 and began their centuries-long rule of Great Britain. During this time, the rulers of the country spoke **Old French** and the peasants spoke English. The peasants tended *cows, calves, pigs* and *sheep* in the fields, which the Normans consumed as *beef, veal, pork* and *mutton.* At least 40% of the words in Modern English came from French, including *air, art, army, court, faith, fashion, antique, sauce,* and *office.*

13th Century — The First Reform
— A monk named Orm began using double consonants to indicate that the preceding vowel was short. A single consonant indicated a long vowel *(holly, holy).*

Middle Ages — Feudal Kingdoms
— Scribes during the Middle Ages copied manuscripts letter for letter, without regard to changes in pronunciation. This tradition was later followed by printers.

— Few people could read or write during the Middle Ages, and because of the many isolated feudal kingdoms, people spoke numerous dialects. Words were spelled as they sounded, and they were pronounced differently in different areas of the country. There were several possible spellings for each word. Acceptable spellings for the word *cliff*, for example, included: *clif, clief, cleove, cleo, cluf, clive, clef* and *cleve*. Pluralization was even more inconsistent, with *cliffs* being spelled *cliffes, clives, cleves, cliven, clifaes, clive, cliuenen, cleues, clyf, clyffe, clyffez, cleoue, clyuen, cleuis, cleef, cliffe, cliuus, kilffe, cleuys, clyffis* and *klyve*. Before 1400, it was possible to tell where something had been written in Britain just by the spellings.

Exploration and Colonization

— Great Britain's colonial expansion into Africa, Asia, India and America after 1500 A.D. led to the adoption of words from around the world. *Coffee* is from **Arabic**, *bandanna* from **Hindi**, *ketchup* from **Malay**, *mosquito* from **Spanish**, *pajama* from **Persian**, and *skunk* from **Algonquian**.

1477 A.D. — First English Printing Press

— Gutenberg's invention of movable type in 1456 attracted the attention of Englishman William Caxton, who set up a publishing house in England. By 1640, more than 20,000 titles had been published in English and a more literate public created an ever greater demand for books. In part because the court was in Westminster, the Middle English dialect of London became the standard for written English.

— Printers did not see any value in consistent spelling at first. They used various spellings of words in order to justify lines of type, and readers were accustomed to seeing words spelled several ways on the same page. For example:

> So it was no bote to stryue, but he departed and rode westerly, & there he sought a vij or vijj dayes, & atte last he cam to a nonnerye, & than was quene Gueneuer ware of sir Launcelot as he walked in the cloystre. And whan she sawe hym there she swouned thryse, that al the ladyes & Ientyl wymmen had werke ynough to holde the quene vp. So when she myght speke she callyd ladyes & Ientyl wymmen to hir & sayd, Ye meruayl, fayr ladyes, why I make this fare. Truly, she said, it is for the syght of yonder knyght that yender standeth. Wherfore, I praye you al, calle hym to me. Whan syr Launcelot was brought to hyr, than she sayd to al the ladyes, Thorowe this man & me hath al this warre been wrought, & the deth of the moost noblest knyghtes of the world. For thorugh our loue that we have loued togyder is my moost noble lord slayn.
>
> MALORY: Morte d' Arthur (1485)

Misspell some words—This wasn't gould.
We owe these printers quite a debt—
Our spelling hasn't recovered yebt!
The vowel shift in men's dialogue
Also helped to make a fogue;
The spelling differences came because
Vowels shifted, and spelling stayed as it wause.
Other spellings also came through
Scholars who wanted to show that they nough
Where words came from (though we doubt
That they were thorough in checking some oubt).
Etymologies often were shown—
This causes modern spellers to grown!
These are some reasons, just a few,
Why spelling may be hard for yew.
But why let old spellings be taught
Instead of changing them, as we aught?
One reason why our spelling's a trial
Is that standard spelling is the stial.
One who from standard spelling is turned
Is classified as being unlurned.
A person who hopes to own a yacht
Must learn to spell, like it or nacht.
Reform would affect a great many people,
From the base of the hill to the top of the steople.
The first reaction will be "No!"
For change is sometimes very slo.
Perhaps someday we'll open our eyes
And maybe we will realyes
The need for change, but until then
We'll have to spell the way we've ben.
But as long as present spelling reigns,
Reading and writing will cause us peigns.

— Sandra Leman

6

*The story of **colonel**:*
*This word came into English through Old French, where it was spelled **coronelle** (and pronounced with an r). The French had adapted it from Italian, where it was spelled (and pronounced) **colonello**. For 100 years both spellings and pronunciations were used until, in a crazy compromise, we settled on the French pronunciation and the Italian spelling.*

*The story of **ache**:*
*In Shakespeare's time, the noun was spelled **ache** and pronounced **aitch**. The verb was pronounced and spelled **ake**. We still see this in pairs such as **speech/speak**. The k was a Scandinavian pronunciation, while the ch was English. For reasons unknown, **ache** eventually adopted the verb's pronunciation and the noun's spelling for both noun and verb.*

*The story of **busy** and **bury**:*
*Dialects varied and words were spelled phonetically during the Middle Ages. We use the western English spellings for **busy** and bury, but the London pronunciation **bizzy** and the Kentish pronunciation **berry**.*

*The mystery of the missing **u**:*
*Until about 1750, people spelled **forty** with a u. Then it just quietly vanished, universally. No one knows why!*

An American GI in Italy is reputed to have found the following sign written with English words. Can you tell what it says? (Answer on page10)

(Answer on page10)

T	O	T	I
E	M	U	L
E	S	T	O

1400 to 1600 A.D. — The Great Vowel Shift
— Our spellings reflect English pronunciation 400 years ago. At that time, the now silent letters in *write, knife, gnat, comb, half,* and *wren* were pronounced. Modern homophones such as *hear* and *here, sea* and *see* had separate pronunciations. On the other hand, *heard* and *hard* were homophones, as were *reason* and *raisin, could* and *cooled.* "Long vowels" actually took longer to pronounce! Unfortunately for us, soon after printing was invented and while spelling was becoming fixed, the vowel sounds of English changed dramatically in what is known as the Great Vowel Shift. The sound in *barn* became the sound in *cat.* The sound in *time* became the sound in *bait.*

1500s — Shakespeare
— Creative spelling was once considered a mark of genius. Shakespeare did not spell his name the same way twice in any of his six surviving signatures, and "Shakespeare" wasn't among those six spellings. More than 80 different spellings of his name have been found!

1568 A.D. — First Call for Spelling Reform
— Sir Thomas Smith published an essay on "correct and improved spelling." Since then, spelling reform has been a frequent topic of public debate.

1600s A.D. — Changes to Reflect Latin
— The English became very interested in classical languages during the 17th century, and changes were made in spellings to reflect their Latin roots. For example, *debt* was once spelled *dette.* The **b** was inserted to reflect the Latin *debitum. Scissors* got a **c,** *island* an **s,** *receipt* a **p.** *Rime* was changed to *rhyme. Aventure* became *adventure* and the **d** eventually became pronounced.

1712 A.D. — English Academy Proposed
— The French had established an academy in 1635 to regulate the language and lay down standards for spelling and grammar. A similar proposal in England was backed by the royal society, the government, and literary eminences. It received little public support. The English resisted all attempts by authorities to regulate their language.

1755 A.D. — Samuel Johnson's Dictionary
— Printers had already done a great deal to standardize spelling by the time the first dictionary was published. In order to organize and alphabetize words, one of several variant spellings of a word had to be listed as the main

entry. The English almost universally accepted Johnson's *Dictionary* as the final authority on spelling, cherishing the volume as they did their Bible and Shakespeare. This stifled criticism of spelling for some 100 years. But Johnson wasn't always consistent: *downhil – uphill, interiour – exterior, amorous – amourously.*

1768 A.D. — Benjamin Franklin's New Alphabet

— Franklin devised a new alphabet with a one-to-one correspondence to spoken sounds. It contained six additional letters. He attempted to interest Webster in the idea without success. Webster initially favored traditional spellings, with a few American twists, although he later changed his mind.

1821 A.D. — Webster's American Dictionary

— Schoolteacher Noah Webster wrote the first American Spelling Book in 1783, and it filled such a need that it went through hundreds of editions and sold more than 80 million copies. This gave him the money and the authority to write his dictionary with revised American spellings: *center* for *centre*, *wagon* for *waggon*, *plow* for *plough*, *honor* for *honour*, *music* for *musick*, *check* for *cheque* and so on. Some of his changes didn't catch on, such as *medicin* for *medicine*.

1876 A.D. — America's Centennial and Spelling Reform

— Spelling reform was popular. The Spelling Reform Assn. and the American Philological Assn. were formed, calling for the urgent adoption of *tho* and *thru*, among other things.

1906 A.D. — Andrew Carnegie and Simplified Spelling

— Carnegie gave a quarter of a million dollars to establish the Simplified Spelling Board. The National Education Association supported it. Theodore Roosevelt ordered that the changes it proposed be adopted by the Government Printing Office. The simplified spelling *tho* (for *though*) was nearly established, but the board pushed too hard with spellings like *tuf* and *yu*. They met with public resistance, simplified spelling became unfashionable, World War I began and Carnegie died.

1950 A.D. — George Bernard Shaw

— Shaw left his fortune to sponsor a spelling reform movement. He wanted an entirely new alphabet, with 40–50 new letters and a one-to-one sound-symbol relationship. This was to be used and taught concurrently with the old system "until one or the other proves fitter to survive."

As an independent nation, our honor requires us to have a system of our own, in language as well as in government. A national language is a band of national union.
—Noah Webster

Noah Webster was a tireless worker for spelling reform. He traveled from printing house to printing house handing out a list of words to be spelled his way. He even lobbied Congress to make deviant spelling punishable by law!

*An intelligent child who is bidden to spell **debt**, and very properly spells it **d-e-t**, is caned for not spelling it with a **b** because Julius Caesar spelled it with a **b**.*
—George Bernard Shaw

Do you like to ghoti?
*George Bernard Shaw once announced that he had found a new way to spell a familiar word: **ghoti**. The spellings of the sounds were from the following words: rough, women, nation.*
(Answer on page10)

8

Spelling Reform — Pros and Cons

The Case for Spelling Reform

It's a poor mind that can think of only one way to spell a word!
—President Andrew Jackson

If you favor reform, you're in good company. So did these famous folks:
Alfred Lord Tennyson
Arthur Conan Doyle
James A. H. Murray, first editor of
The Oxford English Dictionary
Charles Darwin
Noah Webster
Benjamin Franklin
Mark Twain
Theodore Roosevelt
Andrew Carnegie
Upton Sinclair
George Bernard Shaw

If spelling is not reformed, our words will gradually cease to express Sounds, they will only stand for things, as the written words do in the Chinese Language.
—Benjamin Franklin

— W. R. Evans published *A Plea for Spelling Reform* in 1878.

"The working of the Elementary Education Act has given a stimulus to public opinion on the matter which has every day an increasing effect. School teachers, school boards, and school inspectors come forward with their testimony, not in a few cases, but in hundreds, to the effect that teaching our anomalous system of spelling to the children of the poor is in most cases impracticable; and that when the task is in exceptional instances accomplished, it entails either the loss of much other instruction that might be imparted during school attendance, or the sacrifice to indigent parents of a child's possible earnings during a considerable period."

— Benjamin Franklin defended his spelling reform program:

"To either you or me, who spell well in the present mode, I imagine the difficulty of changing that mode for the new is not so great, but that we might perfectly get over it in a week's writing. As to those who do not spell well, if the two difficulties are compared, (viz.) that of teaching them true spelling in the present mode and that of teaching them the new alphabet and the new spelling according to it; I am confident that the latter would be by far the least. They naturally fall into the new method already, as much as the imperfection of their alphabet will admit of; their present bad spelling is only bad, because contrary to the present bad rules; under the new rules it would be good. The difficulty of learning to spell well in the old way is so great, that few attain it; thousands and thousands writing on to old age, without ever being able to acquire it."

— Noah Webster wrote:

"In the essays, ritten within the last yeer, a considerable change of spelling iz introduced by way of experiment. This liberty waz taken by the writers before the age of queen Elizabeth, and to this we are indeted for the preference of modern spelling over that of Gower and Chaucer. The man who admits that the change of *housbonde, mynde, ygon, moneth* into *husband, mind, gone, month,* iz an improovment, must acknowlege also the riting of *helth, breth, rong, tung, munth,* to be an improvement. There iz no alternativ. Every possible reezon that could ever be offered for altering the spelling of wurds, stil exists in full force; and if a gradual reform should not be made in our language, it wil proov that we are less under the influence of reezon than our ancestors."

— The pressure to simplify is increasing because of the millions of people now learning English as a second language and because of computers and mechanical reading and writing.

The Case against Reform

— Although English spellings are inconsistent, they are familiar. Change would cause great confusion, more than would result from a switch to the metric system in the U.S.

— English is spoken by some 700 million people worldwide. It would be a monumental job to reeducate everyone.

— About half of the books in the world are in English. To effect true reform, all would have to be reprinted. Otherwise, people would have to master *two* systems.

— If spelling was changed to reflect pronunciation, whose pronunciation would be used? There are wide variations in pronunciation among native speakers of English and change continues. The word *girl,* for example, could be spelled *gurl* in most of America, *goil* in New York, *gel* in London and Sidney, *gull* in Ireland, *gill* in South Africa, and *gairull* in Scotland. All English speakers at least have a common written language!

— It is much easier to see the need for reform than to devise a sensible system. Spelling reformers have been sharply divided, some advocating a new alphabet and some wishing to adapt the alphabet we have. Here are examples of *The Little Red Hen* using two different systems:

dhe litl red hen
wuns upon a tiem litl red hen livd in a barn widh hur fiev chiks. a pig, a kat and a duk maed dhaer hoem in dhe saem barn. eech dae litl red hen led hur chiks out too look for fuud. but dhe pig, dhe kat and dhe duk wood not look for fuud.

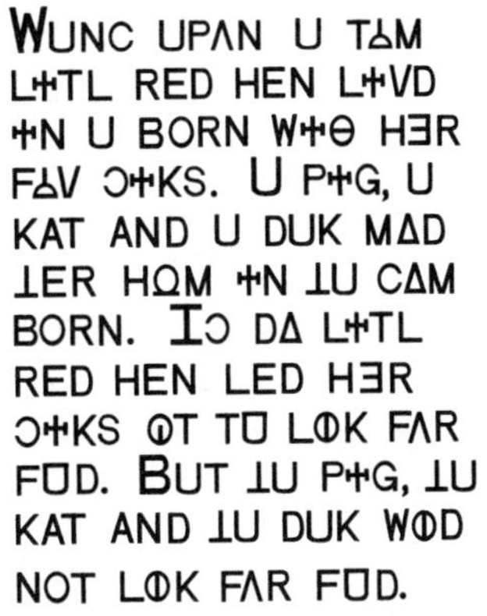

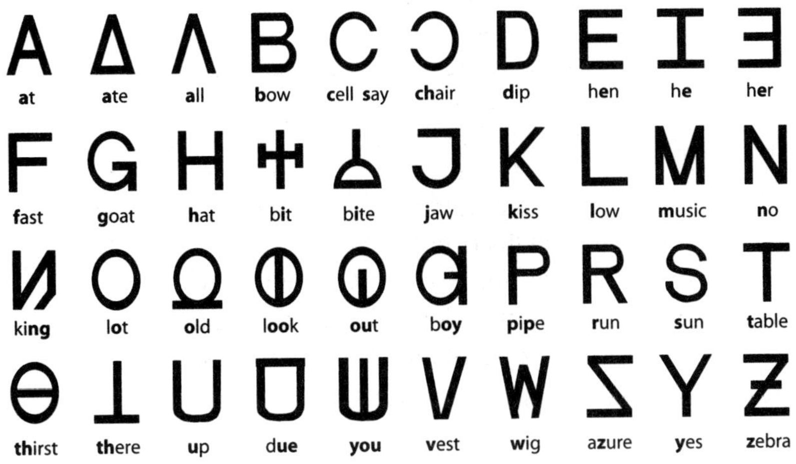
at
ate
all
bow
cell say
chair
dip
hen
he
her
fast
goat
hat
bit
bite
jaw
kiss
low
music
no
king
lot
old
look
out
boy
pipe
run
sun
table
thirst
there
up
due
you
vest
wig
azure
yes
zebra

It is not the sole function of writing to represent sounds. If I receive a letter beginning "My deer sir," I have seen a vision of a horned animal before my mental ear has perceived the sound of the word.
—Henry Bradley, 1913

Because of its mongrel origins, English is especially intractable to phonetic spelling. Eminent and thoughtful philologists have come to the conclusion that the system of spelling English that has grown organically, in spite of its often cited inconsistencies, comes remarkably close to being the best possible orthographic system for so complex a language.
—Philip Howard
The State of the Language

New phonetic spelling would cut off twenty centuries of history of the English language, some of it informative, all of it valuable.
—Philip Howard
The State of the Language

We instinktivly shrink from any chaenj in whot iz familyar; and whot kan be mor familyar dhan dhe form ov wurdz dhat we hav seen and riten mor tiemz than we kan posibly estimaet. At dhe furst glaans a pasej in eny reformd speling looks 'kweer' or 'ugly'.
—Simplified Spelling Society

10

A Drim Kum Tru

If he had not tried to rush it, George Bernard Shaw might have succeeded in giving the English-speaking peoples a phonetic alphabet. Says the *Smithsonian Torch:* "We are in complete accord with Bernard Shaw's campaign for a simplified alphabet. But instead of immediate drastic legislation, we advocate a modified plan."

In 1957, for example, we would urge the substituting of **s** for soft **c**. Sertainly students in all sites of the land would be reseptive to this.

In 1958, the hard **c** would be replased by **k** sinse both letters are pronounsed identikally. Not only would this klarify the konfusion in the minds of spellers, but typewriters and linotypes kould all be built with one less letter and all the manpower and materials previously devoted to making the **c**'s kould be used to raise the national standard of living.

In the subsequent blaze of publisity it would be announsed that the troublesome **ph** would henseforth be written **f**. This would make words like **fonograf** 20 persent shorter in print.

By 1959, publik interest in a fonetik alfabet kan be expekted to have reatshed a point where more radikal prosedures are indikated. We would urge at that time the elimination of al double leters whitsh have always ben a nuisanse and desided deterent to akurate speling.

We would al agre that the horible mes of silent **e**'s in our language is disgrasful. Therefor, in 1961, we kould drop thes and kontinu to read and writ merily along as though we wer in an atomik ag of edukation. Sins by this tim it would be four years sins anywun had used the leter **c**, we would then sugest substituting **c** for **th**.

Kontinuing cis proses year after year, we would eventuali hav a reali sensibl writen languag. By 1975, wi ventyur to sa cer wud bi no mor uf ces teribli trublsum difikultis. Even Mr. Shaw, wi beliv, wud be hapi in ce noleg cat his drims finali kam tru.

—*Time*, May 6, 1957

© 1957 Time Inc. Reprinted by permission.

The following organization is *currently* working toward simplified spelling as one remedy for the problem of illiteracy. Their SoundSpeler computer program translates phonetic spellings input by the user into conventional spellings.

American Literacy Council
680 Ft. Washington Avenue
New York, NY 10040
www.americanliteracy.com

80% of our words are not spelled phonetically. In effect, we have two languages, one spoken and the other written.

—Richard Lederer
Crazy English

We need to continue to evolve an orthography that does not overburden learners of English as a second language, destroy the information other than pronunciation that spelling gives, or outrage native writers of English by its crudity.

—Philip Howard
The State of the Language

Answers:
page 6: To tie mules to.
page 7: fish

SPELLING

AND

TEACHING

How important is spelling? Given that spelling in English is inherently inconsistent, and therefore difficult for most students, what is the best way to teach it in a crowded school curriculum?

Knowing what research says about the memory and about what constitutes an effective spelling program can help teachers make important decisions about their own approach to instruction in spelling and language arts. The goal must be to effect improvement of spelling *in writing*. Unless there is transfer into writing, a spelling program cannot be considered truly effective.

LIKE IT OR NOT, GOOD SPELLING COUNTS

TEACHERS AND SCHOOLS ARE JUDGED BY THE QUALITY OF STUDENT SPELLING

When students "can't even spell," an often incorrect assumption is made that they can't do much of anything! The public expects that children will learn to spell in school, and educators are likely to come under fire for "not doing their job" if they don't.

Historically, orthography was "queen of the curriculum" in Britain. The class system and reverence for tradition were likely causes for the popular resistance to spelling reform. Socially, there were the "men of letters" and the largely illiterate "hoi polloi." Anyone who could not spell was subject to ridicule for being lower class and uneducated. This was a powerful motivation for study!

Vestiges of that attitude remain in some American traditions. The winner of our National Spelling Bee meets the President and appears on TV as a sort of national hero. A foreigner observing this could conclude that good spelling is considered the most important sign of a quality education in the United States.

SPELLING IS USED TO EVALUATE INTELLIGENCE

A person's general literacy and intelligence is often judged according to correctness in spelling. This may seem unfair, but it is so. Employers, for example, may make incorrect assumptions about a person's abilities based on misspellings in letters of application, especially misspellings of basic and commonly used words. Such impressions could keep a very capable person from being hired for a job that she wants and for which she is well suited.

SPELLING IS USED TO EVALUATE CHARACTER

Good spelling shows attention to quality and detail as well as courtesy, important attributes of character. Such courtesy is *expected* by employers and college professors, among others. Literate readers are often offended when they must put forth extra effort and spend extra time puzzling out words because of poor spelling. As a result, the writer's ideas get less attention than they may deserve. People may have the attitude, "Why should we take what you're writing seriously when you won't even take the time to check your spelling?"

Bad spelling is slovenliness and carelessness, like having egg-stains on one's tie.

—Philip Howard
The State of the Language

I must tell you, that orthography, in the true sense of the word, is so absolutely necessary for a man of letters, or a gentleman, that one false spelling may fix a ridicule upon him for the rest of his life; and I know a man of quality, who never recovered the ridicule of having spelled **wholesome** *without the* **w**.

—Lord Chesterfield
in a letter to his son, 1750

Take care that you never spell a word wrong. Always before you write a word, consider how it is spelled, and, if you do not remember it, turn to a dictionary.

—Thomas Jefferson
in a letter to his wife, 1783

POOR SPELLING CAN DISTORT MEANING

Consider the following notes actually sent by parents to teachers. Enjoy the humor, but notice the distortion of meaning, as well as any judgments you subconsciously make about the writers based on their spelling:

"Dick was absent yesterday because of a sour trout."

"Lynda had stripe infection and swallon gland."

"Diana was home Friday afternoon because she was sick and had craps in her stomach."

"Matthew was hit yesterday playing football. He was hurt in the growing part."

KNOWING HOW TO SPELL MAKES WRITING EASIER

Although learning to spell takes time and effort, the payoff is that it eventually becomes easy and even automatic for most people. Writing then becomes a less tedious process, and the writer is free to concentrate on ideas and expression. Less time is needed for proofreading and editing, which leaves more time for revising. Although computerized spell checkers are wonderful tools, writers must still *care* about good spelling and be able to spell commonly used words, especially homophones, in order to communicate efficiently and effectively. Literate people who cannot spell are working with a handicap.

One should not aim at being possible to understand, but at being impossible to misunderstand.
—Quintillian

From the first dictionary up to our own day, the ability to spell according to our conventional fixed pattern has been looked on as the outward sign of a literate man.
—G. H. Vallens

HISTORICAL POINTS OF INTEREST

— *Flour* was once an alternate spelling of *flower*. Both words had identical meanings. Over time, *flour* took on one of the meanings of *flower* and a new set of homophones was born.

— *Surprise* was spelled *surprize* until the end of the 18th Century.

— *Comming* was once a correct spelling.

— The *gh* in *right* and *cough* was once a guttural sound, like that in the word *loch* in Scottish.

— The final **e** in words such as *name*, *stone*, and *dance* was once sounded. These were two-syllable words.

— *Daughter* once rhymed with *laughter*. *Though* rhymed with *cough*. *Mouse* rhymed with *moose*, and *moon* rhymed with *moan*.

— *Quite*, *white* and *wait* were once spelled *quight*, *whight*, and *waight*. *Gifts* was spelled *guifts*.

— Once there were many more irregular verbs such as our *sing-sang*. For example: *ache-oke*, *step-stope*, *climb-clomb*, and *shave-shove*.

Why Don't Schools Do a Better Job of Teaching Spelling?

The Curriculum Is Ever More Crowded

Teachers are expected to teach more and more in the same amount of time. Students often enter class without good work habits or the strong motivation necessary to actually *learn* more in less time. Teachers know that to be effective, they must start from where the students actually are, and proceed at a pace that keeps them challenged but does not leave them confused and discouraged. Because of the pressure to "cover" so much material in a school year, teachers are forced to make hard decisions about what's most important. They have the option of hurrying children through the curriculum, teaching all assigned units superficially. They may omit or quickly "cover" some topics while teaching others in depth and to mastery. They may continue to move on through the curriculum without providing adequate time for review. This frequently happens with spelling. When students are expected to learn 25–30 *new* words each week, adequate time for review is simply not available!

Spelling is considered by most teachers to be important, but not *as* important as reading, writing, science or math. Because spelling is more difficult and less interesting than other subjects, and because of the extreme time pressure in the classroom, spelling may be given "a lick and a promise."

Traditional Ways of Teaching Spelling Don't Work

There Is Little Transfer into Student Writing
A spelling program is working if students' first draft writing is improving. This rarely happens with traditional methods of instruction. James Goss at the University of Oklahoma found that children had studied and "knew" 50% of the words they misspelled in written composition.

Spelling Programs Do Not Agree on Which Words Should Be Taught
A study by E. A. Betts compared 17 published spelling programs. Altogether, they contained a total of 8,645 different words. Only 6.26% of the words were included in all 17 programs. Only *one* word was placed at the same grade level in all books surveyed!

To be successful in spelling, you have to be exact; you must drill and drill, and therefore spend more time than you do in any other skill.

—Edna L. Furness
Spelling for the Millions

The curriculum should not clutter the air. It should clear it for creativity.

— Mauree Applegate
Easy in English

My spelling is Wobbly. It's good spelling but it Wobbles, and the letters get in the wrong places.

—A. A. Milne
Winnie-The-Pooh

Word Lists May Confuse Children More Than Help Them

Spelling texts are generally written by linguists, not teachers. The way words are grouped into lists can confuse learners who are not naturally adept at spelling and who most need instruction. Note the problems one girl had as she struggled to learn a list teaching ways to spell the ō sound.

```
*grown   alsowv
*blow    dunev
vhellow  Sopev
*toad    Pole*
*those   crow*
```

Traditional Spelling Exercises Give Little *Spelling* Practice

Some studies indicate that 40–60% of exercises assigned in spelling provide no spelling practice. Traditional activities such as those listed below may have value for teaching vocabulary, reference skills, or language, but they are *not* effective in teaching spelling:

— Looking up words in the dictionary and copying the definitions.
— Using spelling words in a sentence.
— Dividing words into syllables.
— Alphabetizing spelling words.
— Copying words again and again without careful checking.
— Using phonics to teach spelling beyond the primary grades, or instructing students to "sound out" words.

TEACHERS *WANT* TO TEACH SPELLING EFFECTIVELY, BUT THEY DON'T HAVE THE RESOURCES

Spelling in English will never be easy to teach. The most dedicated teachers face obstacles that may be insurmountable considering the constraints of time and imposed curriculum. *Spelling Plus* was written to provide teachers with resources that will enable them to do as good a job as possible in as little time as necessary. This will free teachers to turn their attention to other important matters, such as creative writing, subject areas, social skills, and critical thinking.

*I can spell **banana** all right, only I don't know when to stop.*
—Primary student

*Samuel Johnson entered the word **soap** in his dictionary under both **soap** and **sope**.*

A college professor once berated a student for his poor spelling:
"You should consult a dictionary whenever you are in doubt. It's as simple as that!"
"But Sir!" the young man replied, "The trouble is that I'm never in doubt!"

There are two schools of thought on the deterioration of student's language skills. One group takes the view that standard English is a 'prestige' dialect and that efforts to perpetuate it amount to an act of repression by the white middle class. Traditionalists argue that our disinclination to teach children standard English—the language of law, politics and medicine—is in itself a fatal form of oppression. Of one fact we are certain, man can't live by incompetence.

—Edna L. Furness
Spelling for the Millions

My mind takes a picture of the word.
—Erica Weston

Is Rote Memorization Really Necessary?

In Spanish or Italian, it's not. In English, it is. Because of the inconsistencies in written English, rote memorization cannot be avoided. Although some students learn to spell without special instruction, most do not. Spelling ability is largely a *talent*, comparable to musical talent. It is not directly correlated with reading ability or general intelligence. The best spellers have excellent visual memory and "see" words in their minds. Some people struggle with spelling throughout their lives.

Although learning to spell well may be easy for some and quite difficult for others, all but a *very* few students are capable of becoming competent spellers with practice. Children should learn *how* to memorize spelling words and how to use the dictionary and other memory aids.

Won't Students Naturally Learn to Spell by Reading?

Some may. Most will not. Reading involves *decoding,* spelling is *encoding.* These are separate skills. Excellent readers may be terrible spellers, and less frequently, poor readers may spell well. Only in the early grades, where the words taught in spelling are phonetically regular, is there a close connection between spelling and reading.

Won't Students Naturally Learn to Spell through Creative Writing?

Writing is creative (right brain). Spelling is critical (left brain). Lindzey and others in their text entitled *Psychology* compare the two types of thinking:

> "Creative thinking leads to the birth of new ideas, while critical thinking tests ideas for flaws and defects. Both are necessary … yet they are incompatible—creative thinking interferes with critical thinking and vice versa. To think creatively, we must let our thoughts run free. The more spontaneous the process, the more ideas will be born…. A steady stream of ideas furnishes the raw material. Then critical judgment selects and refines the best ideas…. Though we must engage in the two types of thinking separately, we need both."

This applies to creative writing as well as problem-solving.

Both types of thinking are necessary, but they are incompatible. When teaching writing, instructors should focus on student ideas and expression, not spelling. Writers must first be concerned with clarity, then with interest to the reader, and *then* with correctness. Nevertheless, the synthesis of creativity and correctness should *always* remain a goal. Poor spelling should not be ignored, nor overemphasized.

The sometimes difficult process of learning to spell should not hold students back as they learn to write. Spelling has no purpose other than writing, and communicating ideas effectively is far more important than spelling words correctly. Instruction in spelling and writing should take place separately but concurrently, with the goal being eventual synthesis.

Invented spelling is necessary, especially in the primary grades, because it frees students to write using words they speak and know but cannot yet spell. Once a student learns to spell a word, it should be easier to write it correctly than to invent a spelling. Invented spelling and misspelling are not the same thing. If a child misspells a word he has studied, the word has not truly been *learned* and should be studied again.

A child who writes an invented spelling hundreds of times may memorize the incorrect spelling. It will "look right" to him. Ideally, children should be taught to spell new words as soon as they are needed in writing. A brand new word will take up to 75 practices to learn, while unlearning an incorrect spelling and relearning a correct one may take thousands of practices. Students should be expected to correctly spell all words they *know* in all writing.

WON'T AN INSISTENCE ON GOOD SPELLING HARM STUDENT SELF-ESTEEM?

It is ineffective to correct or chide students after the fact, or to admonish them to "be more careful." It is useless and discouraging to circle misspellings in creative writing in red. It is inaccurate to equate spelling ability with intelligence or personal worth. The focus should be on encouraging progress and teaching so as to prevent errors. Hold up high standards for students! Be persistent! *Believe* in students even when they become discouraged and lose faith in themselves. Never, never give up! Celebrate accomplishment and encourage peers to notice and compliment improvements. *Especially* compliment students who overcome obstacles to achieve, those for whom spelling is difficult. Self-esteem will be enhanced when students trace their progress objectively and receive the support and encouragement of others.

It is a fact that few people, no matter how literate or well-educated, ever attain real expertness in English spelling without careful training.
—Norman Lewis
Correct Spelling Made Easy

AMAZING MEMORY

THE BASICS OF LEARNING

Learning involves seeking information, remembering information so that it can be recalled, and applying information. Unless information can be remembered, it is unavailable to be applied creatively in problem solving.

For information or a skill to be *learned*, a student must pay attention to it long enough for it to enter the mind through short-term memory and be processed in some way for storage in long-term memory. This happens when it is rehearsed, categorized, or somehow linked to what is already known. Then, retrieval of the information or skill must be practiced over time to ensure that recall is automatic.

SHORT-TERM MEMORY

The mind serves as a lightning-fast processor that sorts through the barrage of sensory stimuli to determine what is important and what is not, just as we sort through incoming mail and toss out what we deem "junk mail." The mind also "tosses" what it considers unimportant. What *is* considered important receives a person's attention. The short-term "working" memory briefly holds information to which we're paying attention at a particular time. It is erased by almost any distraction, and is extremely limited in capacity, holding only four to seven "bits" of information at a time. To get into long-term memory, information must be processed. A reader processes printed words into ideas, emotions or experiences. The words are quickly "forgotten" but the ideas remain. Information deemed important enough to be learned must be rehearsed or categorized for storage in long-term memory.

LONG-TERM MEMORY

Long-term memory is essentially unlimited, as well as remarkably long-lasting. Our brains contain some 100 billion neurons, more than stars in the Milky Way. The number of possible connections and pathways through these neurons is practically infinite, inexhaustible within the span of a human life. No one knows so much that it is impossible to learn more.

For new information to be stored in the brain, it must be coded and "filed." New neural pathways, linking the information with what is already known, must be forged. Then, these pathways must be "traveled" often enough that they are solidly fixed. Finally, the information must be rehearsed or

The true art of memory is the art of attention.

—*Samuel Johnson*

Virtually all learning is based on memory. Educators don't like to admit it, but they know it's true. And any student knows that the more he remembers, the better grades he'll get from the teacher who likes to put down "memorization."

—*Harry Lorayne and Jerry Lucas*
The Memory Book

recalled once in a while over time to prevent the memory from fading. There are two types of long-term memory, declarative and procedural.

— **Declarative Memory** is memory of facts and symbols such as names, dates and events. These seem easy to learn but are easy to forget. Spellings are stored in declarative memory.
— **Procedural Memory** is memory of complex sequences or skills, such as riding a bike or solving a complicated multiplication problem. These are difficult to learn and, once mastered, difficult to forget. The complex process of writing would be stored in procedural memory.

Generally, learning starts at the declarative stage. A student learns facts, rules, sequences and terminology, then gradually integrates and internalizes them as automatic proficiency is attained. This applies to handwriting, spelling, and mechanics in the process of writing. Once proficiency is attained, the specifics are often forgotten. That is why people who have mastered a procedure may have difficulty teaching it. They are not consciously aware of the specifics of what they do.

Information or skills securely stored in long-term memory do not require conscious attention. The working memory is freed to create new ideas or assimilate new learning. If short-term memory is compared to a working desktop, long-term memory is like a filing system.

FORGETTING

When something is forgotten, it has either been "tossed" or "lost" by the mind. People can typically recall only about one of 100 bits of information received by the senses. Incoming sensory stimuli is compared with the memory's store of related prior experience and most of it is filtered out and rejected as unimportant. It is never "gotten" in the first place. It is, allegorically, "tossed." This can happen with names of people we meet unless we make a conscious effort to remember.

Information that we *have* memorized and *want* to remember can be "lost." Visualize long-term memory as a huge filing system with an unlimited number of cabinets, drawers and folders. If new information is simply stuffed into any available drawer with no system of organization or indexing, it *is* in memory but cannot be located, recalled or used. It has been "lost." The more information stuffed and misfiled, the more difficult it is to remember and use *anything* in the memory because of interference.

Researchers recommend that people who are learning a skill frequently observe experts performing it, practice it often, receive continual constructive feedback followed by immediate further practice, gradually increase the number of actions they view as a single behavioral unit, and integrate mastered prerequisite skills into the mastery of the more advanced skill.
—Robert Sylvester
Educational Leadership, April 1985

If new learning is not reviewed within 24 hours, recall drops to 75%. If it's not reviewed within 48 hours, recall is only 25%.

What the Mind Remembers Best

Teachers can assist students in learning to make the most of their natural capacity to remember by taking advantage of the mind's constant search for novelty and for patterns. Emotions can also be a powerful aid to memory.

"Firsts" are relatively easy to remember. They are fresh and novel, and the mind has to create a new category for them.

Once something has happened again and again, the mind sees a pattern and remembers the "general." Thereafter, it tends to remember only what deviates significantly from the norm, the "unusual." Often unusual events are accompanied by emotions such as surprise, anger or pleasure, further aiding memory.

The mind also tends to remember "lasts." It is usually easier to remember where you parked your car today than where you parked it last week, for example. The mind remembers some information until it's no longer needed and then forgets it.

One explanation for the general inability to remember events that happened during the first few years of life is that a young child does not yet know what is usual and what is unusual. Incoming sensory stimuli are stored randomly. A child must build a mental structure or framework for comparing, organizing and storing data before it is available for recall. Language (labeling) greatly facilitates this process.

Enhancing Memory

To enhance memory, learn to capitalize on the mind's search for patterns and for novelty.
— Look for sameness (patterns). What does this new information have in common with something I already know? Especially, look for similarities in things that are apparently quite different from each other.
— Look for differences (novelty). How is this significantly different from something I already know? Especially, look for differences in things that are apparently quite similar.
— Examine new information consciously to determine as many ways as possible to describe, define, or use it. Categorize it and recategorize it. Relate it, link it, or "plug it in" to as many other ideas or facts as possible. The more connections forged during learning, the more likely the learner is to "hit upon" a neural pathway leading to the memory. This is like indexing and cross-indexing information in a book.
— Where patterns do not exist, try to create them. Many mnemonics do this. For example, one way to remember the names of the Great Lakes is HOMES. Each letter stands

The goal is to develop activities that help students learn important samenesses. Such activities should also keep students from learning inappropriate samenesses, and should call attention to unintended samenesses that students are likely to learn.

—Douglas Carnine
New Research on the Brain
Phi Delta Kappan, January 1990

for the first letter of one of the lakes. The letters have been rearranged into a pattern that doesn't naturally exist.

— Where novelty doesn't exist, try to create it. Some of the most effective mnemonics take advantage of this, and memory experts say that the more wild, crazy and emotionally laden a mental "picture" is, the better the mind remembers it. For example, one way to remember the Spanish word *pan,* meaning *bread,* is to visualize a pan with a long loaf of bread as the handle.

INTERNAL AND EXTERNAL MEMORY

Often, information does not need to be memorized, or incorporated into internal memory, in order to be easily accessed and applied. External memory will serve the purpose. It is far more efficient, for example, to have reference materials such as telephone books or appointment calendars than to make the effort to memorize numerous seldom-used details. External memory technology is improving rapidly with computers.

Taking notes is a system of external memory. So is storing information in a filing cabinet or on a computer. Any reference book can serve as external memory, as long as the student knows *about* the information and knows how to access it.

Some facts, however, should be memorized. In general, students should memorize anything with high utility that can be processed entirely within the mind, such as math facts and spellings of frequently used words. Time is *conserved* when a person *knows* that 8 x 7 = 56 and does not need to search for a calculator. Looking up spellings of frequently used words in a dictionary again and again would consume more time than would be needed to memorize the spellings. Educated people are presumed to have basic knowledge *in their heads.* Extreme dependence on external technology is functional illiteracy.

Students should use the most efficient available external memory technology for things with limited utility and things not easily processed in the mind. Teach reference skills, and show students how to organize, store and retrieve their own notes.

SKILLED MEMORY

Experts not only take advantage of mnemonics that make things novel and create patterns, they build and memorize hierarchical structures to which they link new information. What a memory expert has in short-term memory is not data, but pointers to data. Training the memory takes time and effort, but is considered by many to be well worth the effort.

WHAT TEACHERS CAN DO

TEACH WELL AND REVIEW FREQUENTLY

Use a spelling program that *works,* yet takes as little teacher time and energy as needed to do the job. Teach mnemonics and strategies such as overpronunciation that help kids remember. Teach less if necessary and teach it better. *Spelling Plus* was written to make it easier to teach well. **Don't** make the cost of mistakes too high, **don't** introduce too much at one time, and **don't** just teach and move on, assuming students have learned. Review, review, review. Teach for *mastery.* A student who has truly mastered a word finds it as easy to spell as his/her own name. Believe in your students while recognizing the difficulty of their task. Encourage students, and persist with high expectations until they succeed. Celebrate every step on the road to success!

KNOW WHAT RESEARCH SAYS

Research has shown that effective spelling programs share the following characteristics:

Time Needed for Spelling Instruction
— The time spent on spelling instruction each week should be 60–75 minutes (12–15 minutes per day).

The Spelling List
— Spelling words should be taught from lists rather than introduced in a meaningful context.
— Spelling lists should be made up of high frequency words, words most frequently needed in the learner's writing.
— Students should already be familiar with the words on their spelling lists. The focus in spelling should be on *spelling,* not vocabulary development.

Recommended Methods
— The test-study-test method is superior to the study-test method. *Caution: Do not assume a child "knows" a word successfully spelled on a pretest. He or she may have guessed correctly. Words should be studied until they are overlearned and can be spelled correctly at all times.*
— Generally, words should be studied whole rather than broken into smaller constituent parts.
— Teaching spelling through phonics generalizations is highly questionable except early in the primary grades.
— Pointing out "hard spots" in words is not recommended.
— Overpronunciation, bringing the pronunciation into compliance with the spelling, correlates positively with improved spelling: *pe-o-ple, g-host, gu-ide.*

— Self-correction by the learner is the *single most influential variable* in learning to spell.
— Word-sentence-word testing is better than testing with dictated sentences.

DEFINE "SUCCESSFUL SPELLING" FOR YOUR STUDENTS

Although learning to spell will be fun and easy for some and difficult and frustrating for others, all students can become successful spellers. Naturally good spellers are lucky! Ease in learning to spell depends on innate talent including visual memory, over which we have little control. Spelling ability correlates less with general intelligence than do most subjects. Becoming a *successful* speller, however, requires:
— Acceptance of personal responsibility for correct spelling in one's own writing.
— Mastery of the most common and useful words and rules.
— A method for approaching new words that is both systematic and adequate for the individual, taking into account learning styles.
— Independence in using the dictionary and/or other memory aids.
— Recognition of regular and irregular spellings.
— An understanding of word construction (roots, prefixes and suffixes).

CLARIFY YOUR STANDARDS AND EXPECTATIONS

Although teachers will have individual preferences, these are my expectations:
— Students are expected to spell words they know correctly in all writing. If a word is misspelled, it obviously isn't yet "known" and review is needed. Misspelling in creative or subject area writing is not penalized, but misspelled words are collected from writing for restudy until they are learned.
— I do not assume students know how to spell any words they've not studied in my class. If they don't know a word, it becomes a "personal word" (see pp. 38–40) and after study I expect them to know it. If it's misspelled again, it's reviewed again, and again, and again until it's known. This takes a long time in some cases, but persistence pays.
— All final drafts and any writing to be read outside the classroom must be letter perfect. Students use pencils rather than pens in my class to prevent too much rewriting.
— Students must accurately copy any words they can see on their papers, the board, or a wall chart. They should double-check to make sure copied words are spelled correctly.

Steps in the Mastery of a Spelling Word
The word is spelled correctly:
1. On the weekly test.
2. On a mixed review test.
3. In dictation.
4. In final draft writing. Mistakes in the rough draft are caught during editing. This is the level of mastery generally needed for standardized tests.
5. In first draft writing and at all times. It's "easy."

24

PREVENT ERRORS WHENEVER POSSIBLE

In the long run, good teaching will result in fewer and fewer errors being made. To prevent errors in the short run:

— **Teach copying**, and show students how to check and correct early in the year. After copying, they should point to and say each letter in the model, then point to and say each letter in their copied word. This is a difficult skill that teachers may incorrectly assume children have.

— **List words on the board** that are needed for a specific writing assignment (in a subject area, for example) but that aren't important enough for everyone to memorize. Pupils must *copy* these correctly. Gifted spellers may select some of these to study as personal words.

— **Gradually build a list of "priority words"** on a wall chart. Students must spell these words correctly in *all* writing. Start with words like *they* or *said* and add only a word or two a week. Regardless of spelling test scores, a student who continues to misspell words on this short list in his/her writing should not get a top grade in spelling.

— **Get small dictionaries** for all students, to be kept in their desks. I also recommend that each child have an almanac, such as *Facts Plus: An Almanac of Essential Information,* and possibly a small atlas. Such a ready-reference collection gives children the opportunity to learn to use external memory aids such as those used by adults.

— **Build personal dictionaries** containing one page for each letter of the alphabet. A student who needs the spelling of a word while writing turns to the page with the beginning letter of that word and checks to see if it has already been listed. If not, he moves the personal dictionary to a specified place on his desk. This signals the teacher that assistance is needed. The student continues to write. As the teacher circulates around the room, she can easily identify a student who needs help and pause to print the word on the correct page of the personal dictionary. Words in such a personal dictionary are entered as needed and are not alphabetized. Students must scan the appropriate page.

— **Teach students what to do while writing** if a spelling is not known. Perhaps write the first few letters and a blank (*man____* for *manager).* Or write an invented spelling and circle it or write it in all caps (*manejir* or *MANEJIR).*

— **Avoid down time** as much as possible. Students should not stop working when they need help. Raising a hand and waiting wastes precious writing time, destroys a child's train of thought, distracts others and can frazzle the teacher! Have silent signals for bathroom and drink requests that can be answered with the teacher's nod.

Assist Students without "Enabling"

Spelling can be difficult, and students can be lazy. Teachers should place the burden of responsibility for correct spelling on the students as much as possible, realizing that helpful teachers will not be available throughout a student's life. Here are some suggestions:

— Have students **list several possible spellings** of a word to see which "looks right" then check to see which is correct with the aid of a dictionary, the teacher, or another student.
— Have a student **suggest letters** as a teacher helps spell the word. The teacher leaves blanks for any letters not known, then fills them in. This is something like the game "Hangman."
— Select some super-spelling students as **peer aids** and teach them how to assist without enabling.

Show You Care about Kids *and* Their Spelling

Hear and fully acknowledge the *messages* in student writing before correcting the *form*. Notice and comment on any improvements in spelling. It is *because* you care about students, their future, and their education that you insist on good spelling.

Don't penalize students or lower their grades for poor spelling in first-draft writing, but don't ignore the mistakes. Devise a way of noting errors without circling them in red or otherwise defacing papers. Some possible strategies include:

— As you read a student paper, list misspelled words on a **Post-It note**. This note can be attached to the paper when it's returned, to be transferred into the personal dictionary. Or, better yet, the teacher can retain the note and give it to the student on Monday as a source of "personal words." See pp. 38–40 for more information on personal words.
— Upper-grade teachers may use light pencil to **make a check mark in the margin** for each error on a line. When the paper is returned, allow students time to search for and correct their errors, perhaps with the assistance of a buddy.

Look for Patterns, Have Kids Look for Patterns

In most cases, words on a spelling list have something in common. Have students look for patterns as soon as their lists are handed out. Also, see if they can find patterns in the types of errors they make, or in the words in their personal dictionaries. Use word groups to create mnemonics. Teachers should notice and analyze student error patterns and use that information to plan review and write dictation sentences to meet the current needs of students.

*According to David Crystal in his book **The English Language**, there are about 400 irregular spellings in English. 84% of our spellings conform to some general pattern, such as **patch, catch, latch**. Only 3% of spellings are totally unpredictable.*

How Spelling Plus Can Help

The 1000 Word Core List (pp. 42–45)

How the List Was Compiled
— **Word frequency counts** have consistently shown that 90% of running text in English consists of just 1000 base words. These are not the exact words on the *Spelling Plus* list for several reasons. For one thing, such counts are based on writings by adults, not children. Words such as *society* and *circumstance* are frequently used by adults, but seldom used by children. Also, some of the most commonly misspelled words in English are not base words. A frequency count of more than 1,000,000 words entitled *Frequency Analysis of English Usage: Lexicon and Grammar*, listed in the bibliography, was just one source used to compile the 1000 word list in this program.
— **Lists of frequently misspelled words** were also used, especially for words assigned to later lists. A small percentage of "hard words" accounts for a great majority of misspellings by students in grades 9–12. A list from *The English Record* was used as a source of these. The sidebar on page 24 contains part of that list.
— **Lists compiled by others** were consulted, including the Dolch list, the Ayers list, and numerous others. Any word that appeared on three or more lists compiled by others is on the *Spelling Plus* 1000 word list.
— **Lists of student misspellings in writing** collected during my own years of teaching were also consulted.

Advantages of the List
— Although no list is perfect for all individuals in all situations, the 1000 word list provides a **focus** for learners and teachers. Students who have mastered the 1000 core words and who know how to study new words and use the dictionary will be well on their way toward competence in spelling.
— The list allows for **flexibility** among teachers within a school. In a schoolwide program, teachers need not philosophically agree on how spelling should be taught. Teachers may use any approach they prefer, as long as all students *master* the minimum 165 words assigned to their grade level. Beyond that, any words a teacher chooses may be taught. Ambitious teachers may individualize spelling from student writing. The Spalding approach may be used, or any standardized spelling text. *Any* effective teaching methods may be used.

— The list provides for **individual differences**. On average, only five words per week need to be memorized in elementary school, making the list short enough that all students can be expected to master it by the end of sixth grade. Students who find spelling difficult have time for the extensive review and repetition they need. Talented spellers use that same time for challenge and enrichment.

— The list is useful for purposes of **accountability**. In a schoolwide program where students have come up through the grades with *Spelling Plus,* teachers can be confident that nearly all incoming students will *know* (i.e., spell correctly at all times) words taught at earlier levels. Little review should be necessary, thereby **conserving time** for creative writing and other subjects.

— The list aids in **communication with parents** by defining minimum standards and expectations. Parents can be asked to help their children study words at home, especially words from early levels that need review.

WEEKLY LISTS (PP. 46–58)

— For use in a schoolwide program, the 1000 word list has been broken down into seven levels, 10 words for Level A and 165 words for each of the other levels. Generally, these lists progress in difficulty from regular to irregular and easier to more difficult words. Because the most useful, and important words are on early lists, teachers whose students have not come up through the grades with *Spelling Plus* should be certain their students master words on the early lists before moving on. Children can progress through the lists as quickly as they are able or as slowly as necessary, with the goal being *mastery* of the 1000 words by the end of sixth grade.

— For purposes of instruction, the 1000 word list has been broken down into **weekly lists of 15 words each**. Reproducible worksheets for each list are on pp. 62–136. Generally, the words in each list have something in common to aid in classification and memory. It should not be difficult for students to get good grades on the weekly test, but that is just the *first* step toward mastery. Mixed review and dictation *must* take place in the months and years after a word is introduced for mastery to occur.

— **Mnemonics, instructional suggestions,** and **possible personal words** are included with each reproducible list on pp. 62–136. Teachers are encouraged to expand on the basic lists using these resources as well as the Word Bank on pp. 138–150.

KEY POINT:

*The lists are suggestions only. Any word may be taught at any level, and retaught at any other level. Words on early lists are **much** more important than those on later lists. Pretest and start where students **are**. If Spelling Plus is used schoolwide, teachers should make sure students master the lists at the following levels by the end of the year.*

> *Level A — Kindergarten*
> *Level B — Grade 1*
> *Level C — Grade 2*
> *Level D — Grade 3*
> *Level E — Grade 4*
> *Level F — Grade 5*
> *Level G — Grade 6*

PRE- AND POST-TESTS (MASTER ON PP. 59–60)

— **Pretesting.** Ideally, students should be pretested early in the school year beginning with List 1, and the results used to plan review and determine where group instruction should begin. See p. 152 for more details.

— **Post-testing.** At the end of a school year, students should be tested on all words they've been taught, including words from as many early lists as time allows. The results can be included in cumulative files.

— A **reproducible master** is provided for pre- and post-testing on pp. 59–60. This master may also be used for review testing at any time.

RECOMMENDED TEACHING TECHNIQUES (PP. 29–40)

— A **daily practice procedure** provides intensive guided practice on words of the week in 10–12 minutes a day. Directives are in the sidebar on p. 30.

— A **homework procedure** provides independent practice. Directives are in the sidebar on p. 31, as well as in the article for parents on the bottom of p. 156.

— **Dictation** provides distributed practice. In my experience, daily dictation is *essential* if students are to transfer what they learn in spelling class into their personal writing. Directives are in the sidebar on p. 34.

— Using **personal words** will help teachers meet individual needs and teach for transfer. See pp. 38–40.

OPTIONAL RESOURCES (P. 169)

— The **Dictation Resource Book** has dictation sentences as well as easy-to-spell proper nouns for teaching capitalization, suffixes and prefixes for teaching word-building, parts of speech for teaching grammar, and etymological notes for words on the core list. Additional dictation sentences are in the Resources section of the web site: www.SusanCAnthony.com.

— **Homophones Resource Book** may be used as necessary when introducing sets of homophones or assisting students individually to overcome confusion. Mistakes with homophones account for about 33% of "spelling" errors.

— **Personal Dictionaries** are available for use during creative writing as described on p. 24.

— **Handwriting Masters** for D'Nealian manuscript and cursive are available.

RECOMMENDED TEACHING TECHNIQUES

The world is filled with exciting things to teach and to learn! But *time* for learning in school is limited and precious.

There are many possible methods for teaching spelling. Only a few are recommended here because they provide the greatest amount of practice in the least amount of time. These are not intended to limit teachers in their approach to teaching spelling.

Daily Practice provides six guided practices per word per day, each in about 30 seconds.

Homework provides 11 independent practices per word per day, each in less than one minute.

Dictation provides distributed practice and allows the teacher to continually reinforce spellings, homophones, punctuation, capitalization and form. Dictation is the *most essential* method for ensuring that spelling proficiency transfers to writing.

Personal Words provide an optional method for dealing with misspellings in student writing in a way that is effective and non-punitive. Personal words allow for flexibility, and can be used either for extra review or extra challenge.

30

DAILY PRACTICE

Teacher: Look at the first word. Spell and read the word. Point to each letter.
All Students: *(softly out loud)*
n - o - b - o - d - y - nobody
Teacher: Trace the word as you spell and read it.
Students: *(tracing and saying aloud)*
n - o - b - o - d - y - nobody
Teacher: Cover the model. Write the word as you spell and read it.
Students: *(covering the model and writing while saying each letter softly)* n - o - b - o - d - y - nobody.
Teacher: Check from the model.
Students: *(pointing to each letter in the model)* n - o - b - o - d - y - nobody
Teacher: Check and correct your word.
Students: *(pointing to each letter in their written word and erasing and changing if necessary)*
n - o - b - o - d - y - nobody
Teacher: Close your eyes. Spell the word and say it.
Students: *(closing their eyes)*
n - o - b - o - d - y - nobody

This practice routine is repeated for all 15 words plus the five personal words on lines 16–20, if personal words are used. The teacher can dictate five words of his choice for the last five lines of the worksheet, if time allows. These can be review words or words applying a rule.

DAILY PRACTICE AND HOMEWORK

WHY DAILY PRACTICE?

A few talented spellers are able to see a word, "snap a picture" of it with their minds, and spell it correctly forever after, but for most students the process of learning to spell requires repetition and rote memorization. Some research studies have indicated that it takes at least 60–75 repetitions for something new such as a spelling word to "stick" well enough to pass into long-term memory. A word learned *incorrectly* may take 600–2000 practices to relearn correctly.

Daily practice and homework provide enough repetition within the four days of study, Monday through Thursday.

Daily Practice	Homework
Spell and read	Spell and read
Trace, spell and read*	Write, spell and read*
Write, spell and read*	Check
Check	Correct
Correct	Write, spell and read*
Close eyes, spell and say	Check
	Correct
	Write, spell and read*
	Check
*a written practice	Correct
	Close eyes, spell and say

Each student who conscientiously does each step in these procedures gets a total of 17 practices per word per day, only five of which are written. In four days of study, that's 68 practices altogether. I prefer these particular methods because they provide so much practice in so little time. Only about six minutes per word per week are required. Once students learn the routine directives, their minds are free to focus on *spellings* rather than on figuring out directions. *Any* type of practice will likely be effective as long as each student gets 60–75 practices.

INTRODUCING THE PROCEDURES IN SEPTEMBER

Much better results are possible if students "buy in" to this program. I share with them the research background and the reasons for doing everything we do. I emphasize the importance of correct spelling, and tell them that they are "programing their mental computers." I share my expectations and goals, and instill confidence in them that they *can* succeed.

We start slowly and take plenty of time for modeling and precise practice before I begin increasing the speed of the daily activity. I want the spelling period to go quickly and smoothly so there will be more time for interesting activities in other areas of the curriculum. Although I do not especially try to make spelling fun, many students enjoy it very much, because of the immediate objective feedback and the individual attention I am able to provide during the daily practice. Also, they see objective progress and feel good about their improved spelling!

I gradually increase the speed so that the practice moves along quickly. No word takes much longer than 30 seconds.

I make a chart with the directives to post on days when a substitute is teaching. When new students enter the class, I work closely with them the first day and slow the speed of practice slightly. I then assign a buddy to assist them.

After students are comfortable with the daily practice activity, we practice homework in class until they know exactly what to do and can finish the homework in 15–20 minutes.

INTRODUCING THE WORDS ON MONDAY

I pass out the daily practice and homework lists on Monday, along with suggested personal words from which they choose five to copy on their lists for both class and home (see pp. 38–40 for more about personal words). I then have students look for patterns in the list. As a word is introduced, I give instruction, background information, and any suggestions that may help students remember the spellings, such as overpronunciations or mnemonics. Every time a word is written during the week or later in dictation, students vocalize the rule or mnemonic that applies, if there is one. Suggestions for teaching are included on pp. 62–136. Teachers should read and highlight what they find useful. Students can invent their own memory helps if they wish.

Although pretesting is supported by research, I did not pretest on weekly lists because I found that children who guessed a correct spelling on a pretest were less likely to seriously study it. *Overlearning* of spellings is necessary. Whether or not you pretest each week, have all students take weekly and review tests as a way of maintaining mastery and emphasizing accountability.

WHY HOMEWORK?

It is virtually impossible to provide the number of practices most students need to master spelling words during the few minutes of daily practice in class. Homework provides the rest of the practice. The procedure is the same each day, so parents know what to expect. Early in the year, we do the homework procedure in class rather than daily practice until students can do it in 15–20 minutes. It is not difficult to complete in that amount of time if students concentrate, but many children are easily distracted and must learn concentration.

The homework paper that is turned in has each word, including personal words, written *correctly* three times. Incorrectly written words indicate that the child did not carefully check and correct. Wrong practice leads to wrong learning!

HOMEWORK

1. Read the word aloud from the spelling list.
2. Spell the word aloud softly as you point to each letter, then read it.
3. Write the word on your own paper as you spell and read it.
4. Check from the model. Point to each letter.
5. Check and correct the word you wrote. Point to each letter.
6. Cover the word you wrote. Repeat steps 3–5. Always check from the model, not from a word you wrote.
7. Close your eyes. Spell the word and say it.

SPELLING LIST

Name _____

Date _____

1. _____
2. _____
3. _____
4. _____
5. _____
6. _____
7. _____
8. _____
9. _____
10. _____
11. _____
12. _____
13. _____
14. _____
15. _____
16. _____
17. _____
18. _____
19. _____
20. _____
21. _____
22. _____
23. _____
24. _____
25. _____

PREPARING THE WEEKLY LIST

1. Photocopy a *Spelling Plus* list or a list you have prepared on the blank master to the left. You may choose to prepare your own list because you are teaching mixed review words, because your students need shorter lists, or because you want to use cursive not manuscript, another handwriting style, or a typed rather than handwritten list.

2. Optional: Add up to five words of your choice on the lines below the main list. These may be words in the same pattern as those in the list, review words, or words applying a rule. As an alternative, you may use these spaces to dictate five different words each day as time allows. This provides flexible mixed review and application of spelling rules. The other five spaces are for personal words, which students select and copy in those spaces after lists are passed out. See pp. 38–40 for details on how to use personal words.

3. Make a second copy of the list. Fold one copy backwards in half lengthwise. Slip it over the other copy as shown so two lists are side by side.

4. Use this as a master to run a two-sided copy for each student for the daily practice activity. The final result is one sheet of paper with four identical lists (two per side) for each student. One list will be used each day, Monday through Thursday. Use the same master to run half as many one-sided copies of the list as you have students. Cut these papers in half lengthwise so each student has a list to take home.

DICTATION

WHY DICTATION?

Dictation is the single most effective strategy I've found for teaching and reinforcing spelling, punctuation, capitalization, grammar and almost anything else covered in a typical language text with the exception of creative writing. It is an essential link between *instruction* in spelling and mechanics and *application* in real writing. It is also a very efficient use of time. It takes 15–20 minutes to dictate and have students write, check and correct four sentences a day. With dictation and the writing process, I can teach almost anything in the language text so that by the end of the year, students *apply* the skills as they write. Even first-draft writing improves greatly.

KNOWLEDGE NEEDED TO WRITE A SENTENCE

As adults fluent in writing, we often forget how much one must know and apply in order to correctly write a sentence:
— Capitalize the first word.
— Recognize and capitalize all proper nouns.
— Remember spellings of any words needed. For example, a child must recall whether to spell a word with the $\bar{a}$ sound as it's spelled in *came, day, they, wait, great, eight, straight, veil,* or even *gauge.* Our inconsistent spelling system makes this a difficult task.
— Recognize when a word needs an ending and when it's a base word: *pact / packed.*
— Remember and apply rules for adding endings: *hop + ed = hopped, hope + ed = hoped, city + es = cities, lone + ly = lonely.* Remember irregular cases such as *truly.*
— Recognize whether a word is a homophone and choose the correct spelling for the meaning intended.
— Recognize whether a word is a contraction or possessive needing an apostrophe: *My brothers are here. My brother's here. My brother's friends are here.*
— Recognize when a comma is needed and place it correctly.
— Determine the type of sentence and ending punctuation.

All this is necessary to write a "simple" sentence. In real writing, paragraphs, form, and dialogue must also be considered. It would be virtually impossible for a learner to remember all of this while his mind is engaged in creative thinking and writing. It is unrealistic for teachers to expect that he will. Creative thinking is incompatible with the critical thinking needed to remember spelling and mechanics. Even

34

DICTATION

1. **Teacher**: The sentence is: *Mary's writing is excellent.*
2. **Teacher**: Say, *Mary's writing is excellent.*
3. **Students**: *Mary's writing is excellent.*
4. **Teacher**: Write, *Mary's writing is excellent.*
   (All students write the sentence as teacher circulates around the room. The teacher may quietly repeat the sentence if needed. Use this time to compliment individual students on using good handwriting and remembering capitalization, homophones, or spellings.)
5. **Teacher** *(when students are finished)*: Is there anything special you must remember while writing this sentence?
6. **Students**: Apostrophe, using *write* not *right.*
7. **Teacher**: Check your papers. How many people remembered those things? If you didn't, correct now.
8. **Teacher** *(writing the sentence correctly on the board and saying each letter as she writes)*: Capital M-a-r-y apostrophe s Mary's w-r-i-t-i-n-g writing i-s is e-x-c-e-l-l-e-n-t excellent period.
9. **Teacher**: Check and correct your own papers. *(When students are finished, continue with the next sentence.)*

as adults, we generally function better when we creatively and freely brainstorm solutions to a problem, then go back to critically consider each possible solution. Literate adults are able to write creatively and correctly at the same time because they have *mastered* basic spelling and the mechanics of writing to the point that almost no conscious thought is required.

As teachers, we must realize that most children need our assistance in bridging the gap between the creative and critical aspects of writing. I teach the writing process concurrently with spelling and mechanics, but separately. At the same time, I begin to build a bridge from critical toward creative with dictation, and from creative toward critical with personal words and editing:

Personal Words

Editing   *Dictation*

Creative   **Critical**
The Writing Process   Direct Instruction
Brainstorming   Spelling
Rough draft   Punctuation
Sharing   Capitalization
Focus is on *Ideas*   Focus is on *Form*

The goal is eventual synthesis. Teachers must constantly keep in mind that it *is* possible for children to learn to write creatively *and* correctly at the same time. Both creativity and correctness are important, and balance between the two is possible. If a person has no ideas to communicate, excellence in spelling and mechanics is useless. On the other hand, if a person has a great deal to communicate but cannot do so in standard written English, he or she is operating with a handicap. His/her ideas are unlikely to receive the serious consideration they may deserve.

ADVANTAGES OF DICTATION

— Dictation provides a means for extended and mixed review of spellings, especially of homophones. Although daily practice and homework ensure that correct spellings are *stored* in memory, dictation provides the repetition and day-after-day review needed to practice *recalling* spellings when needed in the course of writing. Without such practice, it is unlikely that spelling in writing will improve.

— Students are not asked to think creatively and critically at the same time during dictation. Sentences are supplied by the teacher. The student can focus attention on form.

— Dictation is routine. The process is basically the same every day—familiar, secure, and comfortable. Students' minds are free to concentrate on concepts rather than directions.

— Dictation provides a means of introducing capitalization and punctuation rules one element at a time, including the new element intensively for a while, then gradually tapering off the amount of practice as students achieve mastery. Periodic review can continue indefinitely. See p. 37 for a list of language elements suitable for teaching in dictation.

— Students learn to carefully check and correct their own work. Self-correction is positively correlated with learning.

— Dictation proceeds from oral language to written language. One method of teaching students how to check and correct is to provide sentences containing deliberate mistakes and direct students to find and correct the errors. I avoid this until students are *quite* good at spelling. There's a risk that one child's mind will "snap a picture" of an incorrect spelling, and *that* will be the impression that remains. With dictation, the only mistakes children see are their own.

— Students receive immediate objective feedback. They correct any errors they find without penalty or teacher intervention.

— Teachers can be flexible with dictation, introducing new concepts as soon as they feel confident that their particular students are ready.

— Teachers can lift dictation sentences directly from student writing or use the names of their own students in sentences to reinforce the connection between dictation and writing.

— The 15–20 minutes a day of dictation give long-term results and are a very efficient use of classroom time.

— The dictation paper collected from each child at the end of a week provides me with up to three grades: spelling, language and handwriting.

CONSIDERATIONS

Ideally, teachers should write sentences appropriate for their particular students, introducing new elements as soon as their students are secure with older ones. Writing these sentences takes time. Because schools and students vary so greatly, it would be impossible for me to provide a generic series of sentences appropriate for everyone. But because the planning time needed may discourage teachers from trying this technique, and because *any* dictation is better than none, I've compiled a *Dictation Resource Book* to minimize this disadvantage. The resource book contains sentences and paragraphs to be dictated after each of the lists in *Spelling Plus*. Also included are lists

GRADING DICTATION

— **Handwriting** is graded according to neatness and correct form of letters.

— **Spelling**. I circle each spelling error and deduct five percentage points per mistake from 100% for a spelling grade. Remember that students had the opportunity to check and correct all spellings immediately after the sentence was written. Any student who is careful and conscientious is capable of earning an A. I note any spelling errors on Post-It notes to be studied as personal words the next week.

— **Language**. I circle each homophone, capitalization, or punctuation error and deduct five percentage points per mistake from 100% for a language grade.

of proper nouns for teaching capitalization, helps for teaching punctuation, suffixes and prefixes which can be added to the 1000 words, and parts of speech for the 1000 words. See p. 169 for ordering information.

PLANNING FOR DICTATION

As part of my planning for the coming week, I write four sentences for each day, 20 sentences for the week. Every word from the previous week's spelling list is in at least one of the twenty sentences. I try to include at least one or two homophones each day, with a focus on the most confusing, such as *to, too, two; there, they're, their; your, you're.* Early in the school year, I use only simple declarative sentences. Gradually, I begin introducing approximately one new element a week from the list on p. 37. I include it intensively at first and then taper off as students feel secure with it and can apply it consistently. Once contractions have been introduced, I include them frequently. I do not introduce possessives until students have completely mastered contractions, which may take many months. I include difficult and irregular words such as *people, trouble,* and *coming* repeatedly throughout the year. I notice when words I've taught continue to be misspelled in student composition and work them into dictation sentences.

I allow 10–20 minutes a day for dictation. Students begin their papers on Monday and use the same paper throughout the week, turning it in after Friday's sentences are completed. To avoid the problem of lost papers, students have brightly colored pocket portfolios, color-coded for each subject. Their red folders contain spelling and dictation papers. After spelling and dictation time, they are instructed to put their papers back into their folders and back into their desks. If they *still* can't keep track of their papers, I notify parents and we work together with the child to correct the problem. Responsibility is as important as organization.

What about students who work slowly?

Dictation is a group exercise, and there is some pressure on students who work slowly. Otherwise, faster students would be bored. I gauge when to move on by noticing when *most* students are ready. Slower students may continue to write as the group does steps 5, 6, 7, and 8, shown in the dictation directives in the side bar on page 34. They refer to the sentence on the board as they check and correct their papers. I move through dictation as quickly as possible without overpressuring students. I ask them to give me feedback privately if I'm going too fast for *them* and adjust the speed if necessary.

LANGUAGE ELEMENTS SUITABLE FOR TEACHING IN DICTATION

Things to review and reinforce with dictation:
— Handwriting and general neatness.
— Spelling.
— Correct use of homophones.

Things that may be taught during dictation:
— Capitalization of first word in a sentence.
— Ending punctuation of statement.
— Ending punctuation of question.
— Comma after *yes* or *no* in an answer: *Yes, I would like to help.*
— Ending punctuation of exclamation.
— Ending punctuation of command.
— Comma preceding *please* at the end of a polite command: *Come here, please.*
— Capitalization of names of people and pets (regularly spelled).
— Comma to separate name in statement of direct address: *Jan, have you seen my book?*
— Form of paragraphs. For this, I dictate the four sentences as one paragraph. Students learn to indent two finger-widths from the red margin line, write to within two finger-widths or so of the right edge of the paper, and continue the sentence on the next line *at* the red margin line. After this is introduced, I dictate a paragraph every day for awhile, then taper off to just one per week as it becomes apparent that students can do this easily.
— Apostrophe in contractions.
— Comma in tag questions: *You're coming tonight, aren't you?*
— Capitalization of names of months and days is introduced on spelling lists 43 and 52.
— Comma between the date and the year: *January 8, 2010.*
— Capitalization of names of cities (your city and others that are regularly spelled).
— Capitalization of names of states (easier ones include *Alaska, New York, Texas, Ohio*).
— Capitalization of country names (easier ones include *France, Spain, United States, Chad*).
— Comma between city and state or country.
— Apostrophe in possessives, *not* until contractions are absolutely mastered.
— Apostrophe in plural possessives.
— Commas in a series.
— Comma in a compound sentence.
— Correct way to fold a letter to fit in a standard envelope.
— Letter form, including correct placement of all elements of a letter.
Return address (street address including common abbreviations with periods, city comma state, zip code).
Date (date comma year).
Greeting (comma).
Body. While students are learning correct placement of elements of a letter, I dictate one short sentence for the body (indent paragraph, capitalize, ending punctuation). Later, I dictate one-paragraph letters and eventually multi-paragraph letters which are dictated over the course of several days.
Closing (spelling of **truly** and **sincerely**, comma).
Signature.
— Addressing an envelope. Students fold the letter and pretend that the outside of the letter is the envelope. Correct placement of the following elements.
Return address (name, street address, city comma state, zip code, *no date*).
Address (full name, street address, city comma state, zip code).
— Direct quotations of statements (quotation marks, capitalization of writer's sentence *and* speaker's sentence, comma, period).
The first week: *"This is fine," said Sam.*
The second week: *Sam said, "This is fine."*
The third week: *"This," said Sam, "is fine."*
— Direct quotations of questions and exclamations. Use a question mark or exclamation point on the speaker's sentence, instead of a comma or period.
The first week: *"What's happening?" asked Jane.*
Continue as shown with statements above, then gradually mix all types of quotations.
— Dialogue. After students have securely mastered punctuation and capitalization of individual direct quotations, combine them into dialogue. Teach that a new paragraph must be started for each new speaker, and later that a new paragraph may be started for the same speaker but in that case there is no closing quotation mark at the end of the first paragraph. There is an opening quotation mark at the beginning of the speaker's second paragraph.
— Outline form.
— Word usage: *can – may, lie – lay,* etc.
— Grammar: parts of speech including comparative and superlative adjectives, regular and irregular verbs, suffixes that form nouns, verbs, adjectives and adverbs, etc.

PERSONAL WORDS

WHY PERSONAL WORDS?

The goal of spelling instruction is correctness in *writing*. Students frequently spell words correctly on a spelling test but continue to misspell the same words when writing.

I use "personal words" to help bridge this gap. Each week each student chooses five personal words to add to his basic list. The following suggested sources of personal words are in order of importance:

For all students, especially average and poor spellers:
— Words misspelled on the previous week's spelling test.
— Words misspelled on review tests.
— Words misspelled in dictation.
— Words misspelled in *any* writing by the student.
— Words from personal dictionaries (described on p. 24).

For excellent spellers:
— Words from lists for future levels. Although these will later be taught to everyone, students should not be restricted from studying them ahead of time. The 1000 words must be learned and relearned, reviewed and re-reviewed until they are *mastered*.
— Words from challenge lists which are not included on the 1000 Word List. These can be words from subject areas, such as the names of states, reading vocabulary words or math terms. Sample challenge lists are on pp. 161–162.
— Super-spellers may study very difficult words in preparation for the spelling bee.

CONSIDERATIONS

Although using personal words is very effective, I've not yet discovered a quick and easy system for managing it. It takes commitment and precious teacher time. If you're a beginning teacher or a teacher using *Spelling Plus* for the first time, you may choose not to collect personal words right away. Try it the second year or after you become comfortable with the rest of the program.

Because of limited teacher time, much of the responsibility for keeping track of personal words rests with students. Involved parents can be extremely helpful in ensuring that students make the most of this learning opportunity. I content myself with the knowledge that I am, as a teacher, doing my best by collecting words and providing this opportunity. I encourage students to select important and challenging words, require personal words to be practiced on homework papers, and grade them on weekly tests, but I cannot monitor personal words completely because of limited time.

PERSONAL WORDS FROM STUDENT WRITING

I keep a pad of Post-It notes nearby as I read or check student papers in any subject area, including spelling. I jot a student's name on a note, then correctly print misspelled words I see as I read through the paper. I do not mark misspellings in journals or creative writing, but rather respond to the *content* of the writing. Misspelled words go back to students the next Monday as personal words. I collect no more than ten words a week even for very poor spellers, to prevent discouragement.

I peel off the notes as I finish and stick them to a blank sheet of paper. I add words from other papers throughout the week, and photocopy the page of notes for my own records.

PERSONAL WORDS FOR POOR SPELLERS

I emphasize *improvement* rather than excellence, and don't load poor spellers with dozens of personal words each week. Instead, I choose the most important seven to ten words students have misspelled, from which they select five. Poor spellers may study the same personal words again and again and again. I express confidence that they *will* learn difficult personal words with enough practice. Misspellings may have been practiced to mastery, and it will take a long time to erase and reprogram the brain correctly. In my experience, personal words and extensive review are absolutely necessary if long-term improvement in the spelling of poor spellers is to occur.

PERSONAL WORDS FOR AVERAGE SPELLERS

Personal words hold students accountable and emphasize the importance of correct spelling in writing. I can deal with repeated misspellings in writing without frustration because I have a means of attending to them that is not punitive.

PERSONAL WORDS FOR EXCELLENT SPELLERS

The *Spelling Plus* program provides for extensive review and reteaching. Good spellers appreciate a challenge, which personal words can provide. Their vocabulary often surpasses their spelling proficiency, and misspellings will appear occasionally in the writing of even the best students. These are words they personally need to learn to spell.

Excellent spellers generally have fewer than five personal words a week which I've collected from their writing. They must fill out their personal lists of five using words from other sources: personal words suggested in the lesson, vocabulary words, challenge words, Words of the Champions, etc.

In my experience, many top spellers are satisfied with doing the regular lists along with everyone else. It is easy for them and they excel at it. Some students, however, very much appreciate the opportunity to earn special recognition by taking on the challenges described below. I encourage and reward students who accept challenges, but do not pressure them into doing so.

SPECIAL CHALLENGES FOR GOOD SPELLERS

I offer classroom dollars and special awards or certificates to anyone who masters a special challenge list. Some possible challenge lists are on pp. 161–162. Choose those appropriate for your students or make up your own, with no more than 25 words per list. Tests for these lists can be tape-recorded and taken by individual students when they feel ready. Although I do not encourage average spellers to try these challenges, they may do so if they wish, as long as they do not neglect studying the basic lists. I offer challenges in other areas that may be more appropriate for them. I emphasize that learning the 1000 words is *far* more important than studying challenge words.

OPTIONS FOR SUPER SPELLERS

A child who gets a near-perfect score on pretests in September is given an additional option by private arrangement with student and parents. The parents may pretest their super speller on the weekly list at home and include only the words missed on a personal list. They then help their child select words from other sources to complete a list of at least 20 words. This list is used during daily practice and for homework in lieu of the group list. On Friday, super spellers take the same dictated test as everyone else, comprised of the 15 words on the weekly list and five teacher-selected review words. After that, super spellers have partners dictate their special list. Alternately, parents may administer the personal test on Thursday night, which the child brings in to be graded.

Excellent spellers get 100% if they miss none of the first 25 words, including those I dictate and the first five personal words. I award two percentage points for each additional word spelled correctly. Super spellers can get 130% or better on a weekly test, and an A+ on their report cards.

REWARDS

In order to acknowledge students who master the core words, schools using **Spelling Plus** may wish to provide special awards after the post-tests at the end of the school year. Any student scoring 100% on post-tests up to and including those at his own grade level deserves recognition. Several sixth graders and an occasional fourth or fifth grader may demonstrate mastery of all 1000 words. These students can be given a sweatshirt or some valued award. If teachers have conscientiously taught and reviewed the words throughout the years, most students should be capable of earning these rewards. Learning our crazy English spellings is truly an accomplishment to be celebrated!

SPELLING LISTS

In a schoolwide program, kindergarten teachers focus on mastery of words in Level A, first grade teachers focus on mastery of words through Level B, etc. If students have not come up through the grades with *Spelling Plus,* pretest from Level A or B and begin group instruction with any appropriate list, regardless of grade levels or ages of the students. Focus on *progress* and *mastery*.

1000 Word Core List

Number indicates list on which the word is introduced.

4	a	67	apologize	57	bicycle	42	caught	67	criticism
52	a lot	67	apology	6	big	38	center	67	criticize
54	able	65	appear	29	bird	53	central	10	cry
17	about	67	appearance	8	black	49	certain	19	crying
14	above	69	appreciate	33	blew	49	certainly	7	cut
57	absent	65	approach	53	blood	54	character	16	dark
59	accept	52	April	31	blow	27	cheat	50	daughter
63	accident	55	arctic	18	blue	8	check	13	day
63	accidentally	6	are	38	board	33	chief	39	dead
65	accommodate	66	area	30	body	20	child	26	dear
54	ache	22	aren't	18	book	55	children	39	death
66	achieve	55	argue	20	both	44	chocolate	62	deceive
67	acquaint	57	argument	34	bottom	30	choose	52	December
67	acquaintance	16	arm	41	bought	14	chose	68	decide
46	across	17	around	18	boy	44	circle	68	decided
24	act	16	art	39	bread	45	city	68	decision
58	action	54	article	34	break	8	class	15	deep
60	actual	4	as	34	breakfast	28	clean	60	definite
60	actually	4	ask	54	bridge	26	clear	60	definitely
58	addition	19	asked	67	brilliant	53	climb	69	delicious
46	address	1	at	26	bring	53	climbed	64	describe
64	affect	11	ate	14	broke	53	climbing	64	description
32	afraid	58	attention	50	brother	8	clock	51	destroy
24	after	52	August	41	brought	14	close	59	develop
30	afternoon	50	aunt	29	brown	49	clothes	59	development
32	again	57	author	56	build	20	cold	6	did
32	against	13	away	56	building	66	college	22	didn't
11	age	38	awful	56	built	14	come	33	die
32	air	23	awhile	47	business	36	coming	33	died
9	all	8	back	45	busy	66	commit	61	difference
52	all right	55	barely	7	but	65	committee	61	different
29	allow	10	be	40	buy	60	complete	63	difficult
46	almost	30	bear	10	by	60	completely	36	dining
46	alone	47	beautiful	58	calendar	64	concentrate	34	dinner
26	along	45	beauty	9	call	69	conscience	58	direction
46	already	24	became	19	called	69	conscious	29	dirty
46	although	41	because	11	came	64	continue	65	disappear
46	always	24	become	4	can	69	continuous	65	disappoint
1	am	15	been	22	can't	66	control	69	discipline
40	America	41	before	25	cannot	61	convenient	68	discuss
40	American	29	began	49	captain	30	copy	68	discussion
20	among	29	begin	16	car	38	corner	63	disease
1	an	35	beginning	28	care	7	cost	67	distance
4	and	19	being	38	careful	21	could	10	do
28	animal	33	believe	60	carefully	47	countries	57	doctor
25	another	31	below	47	carried	45	country	19	does
53	answer	61	benefit	45	carry	42	course	22	doesn't
21	any	5	best	46	carrying	50	cousin	7	dog
37	anybody	34	better	28	case	38	cover	19	doing
37	anyway	41	between	37	catch	47	cries	58	dollar

22 don't	59 expect	43 further	39 heavy	2 it
14 done	59 experience	11 game	62 height	22 it's
53 doubt	59 explain	9 gave	18 hello	22 its
29 down	60 extremely	60 generally	5 help	25 itself
24 draw	30 eye	5 get	16 her	52 January
7 drop	11 face	35 getting	13 here	69 jealous
35 dropped	24 fact	29 girl	40 high	66 journal
35 dropping	32 fail	9 give	6 him	52 July
43 during	32 fair	36 giving	25 himself	52 June
51 duty	67 familiar	10 go	6 his	7 just
27 each	47 families	19 goes	14 home	15 keep
47 earlier	45 family	19 going	14 hope	5 kept
39 early	16 far	14 gone	36 hoping	56 key
39 earth	69 fascinate	18 good	35 hopping	20 kind
47 easiest	53 fasten	18 goodbye	17 horse	33 knew
27 east	50 father	3 got	51 hospital	31 know
27 easy	44 favorite	34 gotten	7 hot	54 knowledge
27 eat	52 February	59 government	17 hour	31 known
54 edge	15 feel	35 grabbed	17 house	32 laid
64 education	19 feeling	11 grade	29 how	56 language
64 effect	5 felt	62 grammar	29 however	16 large
62 eight	33 few	50 grandfather	69 humorous	4 last
62 either	33 field	50 grandma	49 hundred	38 later
49 eleven	40 fight	13 gray	45 hungry	42 laugh
48 else	58 figure	34 great	47 hurried	42 laughed
65 embarrass	9 fill	15 green	45 hurry	42 laughter
5 end	19 filled	17 ground	46 hurrying	13 lay
45 enemy	55 final	41 group	43 hurt	28 lead
51 enjoy	55 finally	31 grow	2 I	28 leader
41 enough	20 find	63 guarantee	22 I'll	39 learn
49 entertain	12 fire	56 guard	22 I'm	39 learned
66 equipped	29 first	56 guess	48 idea	27 least
63 escape	9 five	56 guilty	64 identify	27 leave
55 especially	10 fly	57 gym	2 if	5 led
56 etc.	31 follow	4 had	64 imagine	62 leisure
18 even	30 food	32 hair	60 immediate	26 length
18 evening	18 foot	53 half	60 immediately	8 less
21 ever	17 for	4 hand	44 important	46 lesson
21 every	54 force	42 handwriting	54 impossible	5 let
37 everyone	62 foreign	34 happen	2 in	22 let's
37 everything	51 forest	34 happened	63 incident	52 library
37 everywhere	25 forget	47 happiness	61 independence	33 lie
65 exaggerate	49 forty	45 happy	61 independent	12 life
59 example	17 found	16 hard	63 innocent	40 light
59 excellent	21 four	4 has	25 inside	61 lightning
59 except	42 fourth	9 have	39 instead	12 like
59 excite	15 free	22 haven't	61 intelligent	36 liked
59 excitement	43 Friday	10 he	57 interest	12 line
59 exciting	41 friend	39 head	57 interesting	6 list
59 excuse	20 from	26 hear	25 into	53 listen
59 exercise	20 front	39 heard	6 is	53 listened
61 existence	9 full	33 heart	56 island	37 little

9	live	50	mother	17	oh	48	poison	50	relative
36	lived	57	motor	20	old	53	poor	66	relief
36	living	49	mountain	3	on	68	possess	44	remember
46	lonely	9	move	21	once	54	possible	64	repeat
26	long	36	moving	14	one	29	power	64	repetition
18	look	40	Mr.	24	only	60	practical	63	responsible
19	looked	40	Ms.	24	open	60	practically	63	restaurant
30	loose	7	much	61	opinion	48	practice	43	return
23	lose	61	music	65	opportunity	51	prairie	62	rhythm
7	lot	7	must	65	opposite	64	prepare	54	ridge
14	love	10	my	17	or	47	prettier	40	right
31	low	11	name	20	other	45	pretty	38	road
8	luck	64	national	8	our	12	price	30	room
47	luckily	26	near	17	out	68	principal	51	rules
45	lucky	65	necessary	25	outside	68	principle	7	run
66	machine	15	need	24	over	48	prison	35	running
11	made	62	neighbor	31	own	41	private	55	safety
61	magazine	62	neither	11	page	66	privilege	13	said
32	main	50	nephew	32	paid	56	probably	11	sale
11	make	69	nervous	65	parallel	44	problem	11	same
36	making	21	never	50	parents	63	procedure	65	sandwich
4	man	33	new	16	part	68	profession	43	Saturday
21	many	5	next	63	particular	68	professor	24	saw
52	March	12	nice	8	pass	44	program	13	say
34	matter	58	nickel	57	passed	68	progress	28	scare
13	may	50	niece	61	patient	44	promise	36	scared
52	May	40	night	51	pattern	64	pronunciation	69	scene
25	maybe	12	nine	13	pay	43	purpose	30	school
10	me	49	nineteen	67	peculiar	25	put	69	science
28	mean	49	ninety	44	people	58	question	69	scissors
28	meant	10	no	48	perfect	8	quick	28	sea
39	measure	37	nobody	67	perform	34	quiet	39	search
53	medicine	48	noise	48	perhaps	6	quit	28	season
15	meet	48	noisy	48	period	12	quite	20	second
5	men	17	north	48	person	32	rain	51	secret
44	middle	51	northern	68	physical	32	raise	51	secretary
40	might	3	not	58	picture	27	reach	15	see
12	mile	14	note	33	pie	28	read	15	seem
49	million	37	nothing	33	piece	28	ready	15	seen
20	mind	48	notice	11	place	27	real	62	seize
51	minute	52	November	32	plain	67	realize	58	sense
69	mischievous	29	now	4	plan	27	really	53	sentence
8	miss	68	occasion	35	planned	28	reason	63	separate
61	misspell	66	occur	35	planning	62	receipt	52	September
51	modern	66	occurred	13	play	62	receive	69	serious
43	Monday	66	occurrence	19	played	46	recess	21	seven
56	money	66	occurring	19	playing	67	recognize	56	several
20	month	52	October	39	pleasant	65	recommend	21	shall
30	moon	17	of	27	please	5	red	10	she
23	more	8	off	58	pocket	61	reference	12	shine
18	morning	48	office	63	poem	66	referred	36	shining
20	most	53	often	48	point	58	regular	17	short

21	should	47	stories	29	third	36	using	38	wonderful
31	show	45	story	6	this	60	usual	24	word
31	shown	57	straight	14	those	60	usually	24	work
8	sick	15	street	41	though	21	very	24	world
12	side	26	strength	41	thought	33	view	21	would
56	sign	37	stretch	49	thousand	48	voice	42	wreck
63	similar	26	strong	15	three	32	wait	42	write
54	simple	46	student	33	threw	32	waiting	42	writer
55	since	47	studied	41	through	16	walk	42	writing
55	sincerely	45	study	31	throw	16	want	42	written
44	single	46	studying	43	Thursday	16	war	42	wrong
50	sister	68	succeed	58	ticket	16	warm	42	wrote
6	sit	68	success	57	tie	4	was	26	year
21	six	7	such	40	tight	37	watch	31	yellow
12	size	34	sudden	12	time	38	water	5	yes
57	skiing	43	sugar	36	tired	13	way	38	yesterday
35	sledding	64	suggest	10	to	10	we	8	you
15	sleep	67	summary	25	today	27	weak	22	you're
35	slipped	34	summer	51	together	30	wear	41	young
31	slow	43	Sunday	20	told	39	weather	8	your
9	small	34	suppose	31	tomorrow	43	Wednesday	40	(your own city)
12	smile	34	supposed to	30	too	15	week	40	(your own state)
30	smooth	43	sure	18	took	62	weight		
10	so	44	surprise	41	touch	62	weird		
55	social	44	surprised	41	tough	24	welcome		
14	some	35	swimming	56	toward	9	well		
37	somebody	65	system	29	town	5	went		
37	something	54	table	54	tragedy	13	were		
37	sometimes	11	take	47	tried	22	weren't		
37	somewhere	36	taking	44	trouble	23	what		
50	son	16	talk	18	true	23	when		
30	soon	42	taught	57	truly	23	where		
45	sorry	27	teach	10	try	23	whether		
17	south	27	teacher	19	trying	23	which		
27	speak	28	team	43	Tuesday	23	while		
55	special	9	tell	43	turn	23	white		
58	speech	44	terrible	49	twelve	23	who		
26	spring	4	than	49	twenty-one	23	who's		
51	stairs	26	thank you	21	two	23	whole		
4	stand	4	that	57	tying	23	whose		
16	start	22	that's	38	type	23	why		
11	state	6	the	50	uncle	12	wide		
55	statement	18	their	24	under	9	will		
13	stay	5	them	25	understand	6	win		
19	stayed	25	themselves	40	United States	31	window		
35	stepped	5	then	46	unless	38	winter		
9	still	13	there	38	until	6	wish		
54	stomach	13	these	7	up	6	with		
18	stood	6	they	25	upon	25	without		
7	stop	22	they're	7	us	55	woman		
35	stopped	26	thing	14	use	55	women		
35	stopping	26	think	36	used to	38	wonder		

Level A Lists 1 – 3

List 1	List 2	List 3
1. am	1. I	1. on
2. an	2. if	2. not
3. at	3. in	3. got
	4. it	

Homophones by Level and List

Level B
    our / are [8]
Level C
    there / their [18]
    for / four [21]
    to / two [21]
    its / it's [22]
    there / they're / their [22]
    your / you're [22]
    whose / who's [23]

Level D
    hear / here [26]
    weak / week [27]
    to / too / two [30]
    know / no [31]
    new / knew [33]
    blew / blue [33]
    piece / peace [33]
    break / brake [34]
    quiet / quite [34]

Level E
    board / bored [38]
    road / rode [38]
    weather / whether [39]
    heard / herd [39]
    buy / by [40]
    through / threw [41]
    write / right [42]
Level F
    stairs / stares [51]
    since / sense [55, 58]
    passed / past [57]
Level G
    accept / except [59]
    patience / patients [61]
    affect / effect [64]
    principle / principal [68]

The homophones taught in *Spelling Plus* are those most frequently confused by students. Additional homophones are mentioned in the lessons but need not be taught unless there is evidence of confusion. *Any* homophones that students confuse in writing should be taught. The *Homophones Resource Book* contains worksheets and lessons to introduce these sets and many others. See p. 169.

Note: Superscript numbers indicate *Spelling Plus* lists.

Level B Lists 4 – 9

List 4	List 5	List 6
1. and	1. let	1. is
2. can	2. get	2. his
3. plan	3. yes	3. him
4. hand	4. red	4. big
5. stand	5. led	5. did
6. man	6. men	6. win
7. than	7. end	7. sit
8. that	8. went	8. quit
9. last	9. then	9. wish
10. as	10. them	10. with
11. ask	11. best	11. list
12. had	12. felt	12. this
13. has	13. help	13. the
14. was	14. next	14. they
15. a	15. kept	15. are

List 7	List 8	List 9
1. hot	1. back	1. all
2. lot	2. black	2. call
3. dog	3. check	3. small
4. cost	4. sick	4. well
5. stop	5. clock	5. tell
6. drop	6. luck	6. fill
7. us	7. quick	7. will
8. up	8. off	8. still
9. but	9. class	9. full
10. cut	10. pass	10. have
11. run	11. less	11. gave
12. just	12. miss	12. give
13. must	13. you	13. live
14. much	14. your	14. five
15. such	15. our	15. move

Level B Lists 10 – 14

List 10
1. go
2. no
3. so
4. do
5. to
6. be
7. he
8. me
9. we
10. she
11. by
12. my
13. try
14. cry
15. fly

List 11
1. came
2. same
3. name
4. game
5. ate
6. state
7. age
8. page
9. take
10. make
11. made
12. grade
13. sale
14. face
15. place

List 12
1. time
2. nine
3. line
4. shine
5. nice
6. price
7. life
8. quite
9. like
10. mile
11. smile
12. fire
13. wide
14. side
15. size

List 13
1. day
2. may
3. pay
4. lay
5. way
6. away
7. gray
8. play
9. stay
10. say
11. said
12. were
13. here
14. there
15. these

List 14
1. home
2. hope
3. note
4. chose
5. close
6. those
7. broke
8. love
9. above
10. some
11. come
12. one
13. done
14. gone
15. use

Level C Lists 15 – 20

List 15
1. free
2. three
3. see
4. seem
5. seen
6. green
7. deep
8. sleep
9. keep
10. street
11. meet
12. week
13. feel
14. need
15. been

List 16
1. car
2. far
3. dark
4. hard
5. arm
6. warm
7. war
8. art
9. part
10. start
11. large
12. talk
13. walk
14. want
15. her

List 17
1. or
2. for
3. north
4. short
5. horse
6. house
7. out
8. about
9. around
10. found
11. ground
12. south
13. hour
14. oh
15. of

List 18
1. took
2. look
3. book
4. stood
5. foot
6. good
7. goodbye
8. hello
9. even
10. evening
11. morning
12. blue
13. true
14. boy
15. their

List 19
1. asked
2. called
3. looked
4. played
5. stayed
6. filled
7. doing
8. going
9. playing
10. trying
11. crying
12. being
13. feeling
14. goes
15. does

List 20
1. old
2. cold
3. told
4. both
5. most
6. find
7. mind
8. kind
9. child
10. second
11. month
12. among
13. front
14. from
15. other

Level C Lists 21 – 25

List 21
1. once
2. four
3. two
4. six
5. seven
6. any
7. many
8. never
9. ever
10. every
11. very
12. would
13. could
14. should
15. shall

List 22
1. its
2. it's
3. that's
4. let's
5. I'll
6. I'm
7. they're
8. you're
9. can't
10. don't
11. didn't
12. doesn't
13. aren't
14. weren't
15. haven't

List 23
1. who
2. who's
3. whose
4. lose
5. why
6. what
7. when
8. where
9. which
10. whether
11. white
12. while
13. awhile
14. whole
15. more

List 24
1. act
2. fact
3. saw
4. draw
5. work
6. word
7. world
8. only
9. open
10. over
11. under
12. after
13. become
14. became
15. welcome

List 25
1. itself
2. himself
3. themselves
4. into
5. upon
6. forget
7. maybe
8. cannot
9. today
10. inside
11. outside
12. without
13. understand
14. another
15. put

Level D Lists 26 – 31

List 26
1. along
2. long
3. length
4. strong
5. strength
6. spring
7. bring
8. thing
9. think
10. thank you
11. year
12. near
13. hear
14. dear
15. clear

List 27
1. weak
2. speak
3. each
4. reach
5. teach
6. teacher
7. eat
8. cheat
9. easy
10. east
11. least
12. please
13. leave
14. real
15. really

List 28
1. sea
2. season
3. reason
4. lead
5. leader
6. clean
7. team
8. mean
9. meant
10. read
11. ready
12. case
13. care
14. scare
15. animal

List 29
1. now
2. how
3. however
4. down
5. brown
6. town
7. allow
8. power
9. dirty
10. bird
11. girl
12. third
13. first
14. begin
15. began

List 30
1. too
2. loose
3. food
4. moon
5. soon
6. room
7. smooth
8. school
9. afternoon
10. choose
11. eye
12. body
13. copy
14. wear
15. bear

List 31
1. own
2. know
3. known
4. show
5. shown
6. blow
7. slow
8. grow
9. throw
10. low
11. below
12. follow
13. yellow
14. window
15. tomorrow

52

Level D Lists 32 – 36

List 32
1. wait
2. waiting
3. rain
4. plain
5. main
6. paid
7. laid
8. fail
9. again
10. against
11. afraid
12. air
13. fair
14. hair
15. raise

List 33
1. new
2. knew
3. few
4. blew
5. threw
6. view
7. die
8. died
9. lie
10. believe
11. pie
12. piece
13. field
14. chief
15. heart

List 34
1. better
2. matter
3. gotten
4. dinner
5. summer
6. sudden
7. happen
8. happened
9. suppose
10. supposed to
11. bottom
12. great
13. break
14. breakfast
15. quiet

List 35
1. stepped
2. slipped
3. grabbed
4. planned
5. planning
6. dropped
7. dropping
8. stopped
9. stopping
10. hopping
11. getting
12. running
13. sledding
14. swimming
15. beginning

List 36
1. tired
2. scared
3. liked
4. lived
5. used to
6. using
7. shining
8. dining
9. taking
10. making
11. moving
12. giving
13. living
14. hoping
15. coming

Level E Lists 37 – 42

List 37
1. nobody
2. nothing
3. anyway
4. anybody
5. everyone
6. everything
7. everywhere
8. somebody
9. something
10. somewhere
11. sometimes
12. catch
13. watch
14. stretch
15. little

List 38
1. cover
2. later
3. center
4. corner
5. water
6. winter
7. wonder
8. wonderful
9. careful
10. awful
11. until
12. yesterday
13. type
14. road
15. board

List 39
1. weather
2. measure
3. heavy
4. head
5. bread
6. dead
7. death
8. instead
9. pleasant
10. search
11. heard
12. early
13. earth
14. learn
15. learned

List 40
1. fight
2. light
3. might
4. night
5. right
6. tight
7. high
8. Mr.
9. Ms.
10. (your city)
11. (your state)
12. America
13. American
14. United States
15. buy

List 41
1. bought
2. brought
3. thought
4. though
5. through
6. enough
7. tough
8. touch
9. young
10. group
11. before
12. because
13. between
14. private
15. friend

List 42
1. write
2. writer
3. writing
4. handwriting
5. wrote
6. wrong
7. wreck
8. written
9. laugh
10. laughed
11. laughter
12. caught
13. taught
14. course
15. fourth

Level E Lists 43 – 47

List 43
1. Sunday
2. Monday
3. Tuesday
4. Wednesday
5. Thursday
6. Friday
7. Saturday
8. hurt
9. turn
10. return
11. during
12. purpose
13. further
14. sure
15. sugar

List 44
1. circle
2. single
3. middle
4. people
5. chocolate
6. favorite
7. trouble
8. terrible
9. remember
10. important
11. surprise
12. surprised
13. program
14. problem
15. promise

List 45
1. busy
2. city
3. story
4. enemy
5. hungry
6. country
7. lucky
8. study
9. sorry
10. carry
11. hurry
12. happy
13. pretty
14. family
15. beauty

List 46
1. always
2. almost
3. already
4. although
5. alone
6. lonely
7. across
8. unless
9. recess
10. address
11. lesson
12. carrying
13. hurrying
14. studying
15. student

List 47
1. cries
2. countries
3. families
4. stories
5. tried
6. hurried
7. carried
8. studied
9. prettier
10. earlier
11. easiest
12. luckily
13. happiness
14. business
15. beautiful

Level F Lists 48 – 53

List 48
1. noise
2. noisy
3. point
4. voice
5. poison
6. prison
7. person
8. period
9. perhaps
10. perfect
11. else
12. idea
13. office
14. notice
15. practice

List 49
1. mountain
2. captain
3. certain
4. certainly
5. entertain
6. eleven
7. twelve
8. twenty-one
9. forty
10. nineteen
11. ninety
12. hundred
13. thousand
14. million
15. clothes

List 50
1. sister
2. mother
3. brother
4. father
5. grandfather
6. grandma
7. daughter
8. son
9. parents
10. uncle
11. aunt
12. cousin
13. niece
14. nephew
15. relative

List 51
1. stairs
2. prairie
3. duty
4. rules
5. minute
6. secret
7. secretary
8. hospital
9. enjoy
10. destroy
11. together
12. forest
13. northern
14. modern
15. pattern

List 52
1. January
2. February
3. March
4. April
5. May
6. June
7. July
8. August
9. September
10. October
11. November
12. December
13. library
14. a lot
15. all right

List 53
1. sentence
2. often
3. fasten
4. listen
5. listened
6. doubt
7. climb
8. climbed
9. climbing
10. answer
11. half
12. blood
13. poor
14. central
15. medicine

Level F Lists 54 – 58

List 54
1. ridge
2. bridge
3. edge
4. knowledge
5. able
6. table
7. simple
8. article
9. possible
10. impossible
11. ache
12. stomach
13. character
14. tragedy
15. force

List 55
1. woman
2. women
3. children
4. final
5. finally
6. social
7. special
8. especially
9. since
10. sincerely
11. barely
12. safety
13. statement
14. argue
15. arctic

List 56
1. several
2. toward
3. probably
4. language
5. guess
6. guard
7. guilty
8. built
9. build
10. building
11. island
12. sign
13. key
14. money
15. etc.

List 57
1. tie
2. tying
3. author
4. motor
5. doctor
6. argument
7. truly
8. interest
9. interesting
10. skiing
11. passed
12. straight
13. absent
14. gym
15. bicycle

List 58
1. sense
2. pocket
3. ticket
4. nickel
5. figure
6. picture
7. speech
8. regular
9. dollar
10. calendar
11. question
12. direction
13. action
14. addition
15. attention

Level G Lists 59 – 64

List 59
1. accept
2. except
3. excellent
4. excuse
5. excite
6. exciting
7. excitement
8. example
9. exercise
10. experience
11. explain
12. expect
13. develop
14. development
15. government

List 60
1. carefully
2. complete
3. completely
4. extremely
5. definite
6. definitely
7. actual
8. actually
9. usual
10. usually
11. practical
12. practically
13. generally
14. immediate
15. immediately

List 61
1. music
2. misspell
3. magazine
4. lightning
5. opinion
6. benefit
7. different
8. difference
9. patient
10. intelligent
11. independent
12. independence
13. reference
14. existence
15. convenient

List 62
1. eight
2. weight
3. height
4. neighbor
5. leisure
6. either
7. neither
8. deceive
9. receive
10. receipt
11. seize
12. weird
13. foreign
14. rhythm
15. grammar

List 63
1. incident
2. accident
3. accidentally
4. escape
5. innocent
6. difficult
7. guarantee
8. procedure
9. responsible
10. separate
11. restaurant
12. similar
13. particular
14. poem
15. disease

List 64
1. affect
2. effect
3. suggest
4. prepare
5. continue
6. imagine
7. concentrate
8. education
9. national
10. describe
11. description
12. repeat
13. repetition
14. pronunciation
15. identify

Level G Lists 65 – 69

List 65
1. approach
2. opportunity
3. necessary
4. recommend
5. appear
6. disappear
7. disappoint
8. exaggerate
9. accommodate
10. committee
11. embarrass
12. opposite
13. parallel
14. sandwich
15. system

List 66
1. college
2. privilege
3. achieve
4. relief
5. control
6. commit
7. occur
8. occurring
9. occurred
10. occurrence
11. equipped
12. referred
13. area
14. journal
15. machine

List 67
1. summary
2. apology
3. apologize
4. realize
5. recognize
6. criticize
7. criticism
8. perform
9. distance
10. acquaint
11. acquaintance
12. appearance
13. brilliant
14. peculiar
15. familiar

List 68
1. principle
2. principal
3. physical
4. decide
5. decided
6. decision
7. occasion
8. success
9. succeed
10. profession
11. professor
12. possess
13. progress
14. discuss
15. discussion

List 69
1. scene
2. fascinate
3. discipline
4. scissors
5. science
6. conscience
7. conscious
8. nervous
9. jealous
10. serious
11. humorous
12. continuous
13. mischievous
14. delicious
15. appreciate

SPELLING TEST

Name

Date

1.

2.

3.

4.

5.

6.

7.

8.

9.

10.

11.

12.

13.

14.

15.

16.

17.

18.

19.

20.

21.

22.

23.

24.

25.

26.

27.

28.

29.

30.

31.

32.

33.

34.

35.

36.

37.

38.

39.

40.

41.

42.

43.

44.

45.

46.

47.

48.

49.

50.

51.

52.

53.

54.

55.

56.

57.

58.

59.

60.

61.

62.

63.

64.

65.

66.

67.

68.

69.

70.

71.

72.

73.

74.

75.

76.

77.

78.

79.

80.

81.

82.	110.	138.
83.	111.	139.
84.	112.	140.
85.	113.	141.
86.	114.	142.
87.	115.	143.
88.	116.	144.
89.	117.	145.
90.	118.	146.
91.	119.	147.
92.	120.	148.
93.	121.	149.
94.	122.	150.
95.	123.	151.
96.	124.	152.
97.	125.	153.
98.	126.	154.
99.	127.	155.
100.	128.	156.
101.	129.	157.
102.	130.	158.
103.	131.	159.
104.	132.	160.
105.	133.	161.
106.	134.	162.
107.	135.	163.
108.	136.	164.
109.	137.	165.

Pretesting, Review Testing, Post-Testing

The reproducible master on pp. 59–60 may be run two-sided and used for pretesting, review testing, or post-testing. Pretests are provided before the lessons for each level, with list numbers noted. See p. 152 for more suggestions about pretesting and compiling group and individual review lists of missed words.

Although pretesting and checking papers at the beginning of each school year is time-consuming, I know of no better way to diagnose individual needs and determine where group instruction should begin. Words on early lists are *much* more important than words on later lists. Begin group instruction at the point where a lot of students are missing a lot of words. That will likely be between Lists 26 and 36, regardless of the age of the students. Focus on *progress* and *mastery*.

During the year, periodically retest students on earlier lists and have them restudy any words missed.

Spelling Rules

The following rules in English spelling have very few exceptions:

1. The letter **q** is always followed by a **u** in English words. (**quite**, **question**) [6]
2. English words do not end with the letter **v**. (**gave**, **have**) [9]
3. When a one-syllable word ends with a short vowel and a single consonant, double the final consonant before adding a suffix beginning with a vowel. (**swim + -ing** is **swimming**)
   In a two-syllable word, double the final consonant only if the word is accented on the last syllable. (**begín + -ing** is **beginning** but **ópen + -ing** is **opening**) [35]
4. When a word ends in silent **e**, drop the **e** before adding a suffix beginning with a vowel. (**make + -ing** is **making**) [36]
   Keep the silent **e** before adding a suffix beginning with a consonant. (**time + -ly** is **timely**)
5. When a word ends in a consonant and **y**, change the **y** to **i** before adding a suffix, unless the suffix begins with **i**. (**happy + -ly** is **happily**, but **hurry + -ing** is **hurrying**) [47]
   When a word ends in a vowel and **y**, do not change the **y** to **i**. (**play + -ed** is **played**)
6. Capitalize proper nouns. [40]
7. Write **i** before **e** except after **c**, or when sounded like **-ay** as in **neighbor** and **weigh**. This rule doesn't apply when **ci** is pronounced **sh** as in **ancient**. [33, 62, 69]

Note: The superscript numbers indicate *Spelling Plus* lists.

Spelling Guidelines

1. **k** or **c** — **k** is used before short **e** and short **i** in one-syllable words. **c** is used before short **a**, **o**, and **u** in one-syllable words. [1, 2]
2. To pluralize many nouns ending with a single **f** or **fe**, change the **f** to **v** and add **-es**. [25]
3. Add **-es** rather than **-s** to words ending with the sound of **s**, **x**, **z**, **sh**, or **ch**. [37]
4. **-ize**, **-ise** or **-yze** — Most common words end with **-ize**. **Surprise**, **exercise** and **revise** are common two-syllable words that end with **-ise**. **Paralyze** and **analyze** are the only common words ending with **-yze**. [44, 67]
5. **-ary** or **-ery** — Most common words end with **-ary** rather than **-ery**, with the exception of **cemetery** and **stationery**. [51, 65]
6. **-able** or **-ible** — The suffix **-able** is more common than **-ible**. **-ible** is generally not added to a whole word. **-ible** is used to keep **c** or **g** soft (**eligible**, **invincible**). Since **notice** is a whole word, **-able** is added. **Noticeable** retains its **e** to keep the **c** soft. **-ible** is used if a related word ends in **-ion** (**collection / collectible**). [54, 63]
7. **-le**, **-el** or **-al** — **-le** is more common at the end of a word than **-el** or **-al**. [58, 60]
8. **-ence** or **-ance** — If the base word ends with **-ent**, **-ence** is correct. If the base word ends with **-ant**, **-ance** is correct. [61]
9. **-cede**, **-ceed** or **-sede** — **-cede** is the most common spelling of this root. Three words end with **-ceed**: **succeed**, **proceed**, and **exceed**. Only **supersede** ends with **-sede**. [68]

SPELLING LIST 1

Name

1. am

2. an

3. at

List 1
Level A, List 1

Words in Patterns:
— Short **a**, Word Bank p. 138.
Guideline for extension words below:
  k *is generally used before short* **e** *and short* **i** *in one-syllable words.*
  c *is generally used before short* **a**, **o**, *and* **u** *in one-syllable words.*

Extension:
— Dictate rhyming words from the following lists. If you use the names, make sure students capitalize them.

am		an		at	
ham	cram	ban	bran	bat	brat
jam	slam	can	plan	cat	chat
ram	swam	fan	than	fat	flat
yam		man		hat	that
Pam		pan		mat	
Sam		ran		pat	
		tan		rat	
		ran		sat	
		Dan		Nat	
		Jan			
		Nan			

— *Caution:* An irregular spelling with the short **a** sound is **lamb**.
— Dictate any regularly spelled, one-syllable words with the short **a** sound.

List 2   Level A, List 2

Name

1. I

2. if

3. in

4. it

Words in Patterns:
— Short **i**, Word Bank p. 140.
Guideline for extension words below:
  k is generally used before short **e** and
    short **i** in one-syllable words.
  c is generally used before short **a**, **o**, and
    u in one-syllable words.

Notes to the Teacher:
— The word **I** must always be capitalized.
This began long ago, when manuscripts
were handwritten. The small **i** was
likely to be lost or attached to another
word. A capital **I** helped keep it a
distinct and separate word.
— **If** is an unusual spelling. Rhyming
words generally end in **-iff** as in **sniff**
and **stiff**.
— Children may say **bin** for **been**, **pin**
for **pen**, and **tin** for **ten**, which will
cause confusion with these spellings.
Pronounce the vowels carefully.

Extension:
— Dictate rhyming words from the
following lists.

in		**it**	
fin	chin	bit	quit
pin	grin	fit	spit
sin	shin	hit	
tin	skin	kit	
win	spin	lit	
	thin	pit	
		sit	
		wit	

— Dictate any regularly spelled one-
syllable words with the short **i** sound.
— Mix dictation of all words on this list
and List 1 as soon as students are ready.

SPELLING LIST 3

Name

1. on

2. not

3. got

List 3   Level A, List 3

Words in Patterns:
— Short **o**, Word Bank p. 141.

Notes to the Teacher:
— *Caution:* The short **o** sound has a number of irregular spellings in common words, such as **gone**, **John**, **yawn**, **bought**, **brought**, **fought**, **thought**, **caught**, **taught**, and **swat**. (The **gh** was originally pronounced as a guttural sound. Words containing it have not always rhymed with **not**.)

Extension:
— Dictate rhyming words from the following lists. If you use the names, make sure students capitalize them.

on	not / got	
Don	dot	blot
Ron	hot	plot
	jot	shot
	lot	slot
	pot	spot
	rot	

— Dictate any regularly spelled one-syllable words with the short **o** sound.
— Mix dictation of all words on lists 1, 2, and 3 and of other words in the same patterns.

Level B Test

The emphasis in Level B is on regular, one-syllable words with short and long vowels (**hop**, **hope**), as well as on commonly used irregular words (**they**, **was**). Adding **-s** to base words is introduced.

1. cut [7]	43. away [13]	84. said [13]	125. come [14]
2. fire [12]	44. that [4]	85. pass [8]	126. your [8]
3. and [4]	45. five [9]	86. sale [11]	127. nice [12]
4. will [9]	46. did [6]	87. with [6]	128. lot [7]
5. end [5]	47. page [11]	88. chose [14]	129. by [10]
6. came [11]	48. clock [8]	89. let [5]	130. then [5]
7. must [7]	49. hope [14]	90. do [10]	131. gone [14]
8. size [12]	50. ask [4]	91. broke [14]	132. call [9]
9. hand [4]	51. stay [13]	92. the [6]	133. stop [7]
10. have [9]	52. quit [6]	93. time [12]	134. cry [10]
11. is [6]	53. made [11]	94. he [10]	135. quite [12]
12. game [11]	54. fill [9]	95. red [5]	136. felt [5]
13. back [8]	55. smile [12]	96. some [14]	137. tell [9]
14. way [13]	56. but [7]	97. you [8]	138. grade [11]
15. than [4]	57. lay [13]	98. shine [12]	139. class [8]
16. live [9]	58. these [13]	99. hot [7]	140. so [10]
17. big [6]	59. just [7]	100. she [10]	141. a [4]
18. age [11]	60. side [12]	101. went [5]	142. here [13]
19. sick [8]	61. plan [4]	102. done [14]	143. miss [8]
20. home [14]	62. full [9]	103. all [9]	144. place [11]
21. as [4]	63. kept [5]	104. cost [7]	145. this [6]
22. play [13]	64. name [11]	105. try [10]	146. those [14]
23. sit [6]	65. such [7]	106. life [12]	147. yes [5]
24. make [11]	66. may [13]	107. best [5]	148. be [10]
25. quick [8]	67. man [4]	108. well [9]	149. above [14]
26. mile [12]	68. give [9]	109. us [7]	150. are [6]
27. up [7]	69. him [6]	110. off [8]	151. line [12]
28. pay [13]	70. state [11]	111. no [10]	152. we [10]
29. there [13]	71. check [8]	112. was [4]	153. men [5]
30. run [7]	72. gray [13]	113. were [13]	154. one [14]
31. wide [12]	73. last [4]	114. less [8]	155. our [8]
32. can [4]	74. move [9]	115. face [11]	156. price [12]
33. still [9]	75. win [6]	116. list [6]	157. dog [7]
34. next [5]	76. take [11]	117. close [14]	158. my [10]
35. same [11]	77. luck [8]	118. get [5]	159. them [5]
36. much [7]	78. note [14]	119. to [10]	160. use [14]
37. day [13]	79. had [4]	120. love [14]	161. small [9]
38. stand [4]	80. say [13]	121. they [6]	162. drop [7]
39. gave [9]	81. wish [6]	122. nine [12]	163. fly [10]
40. his [6]	82. go [10]	123. me [10]	164. like [12]
41. ate [11]	83. has [4]	124. led [5]	165. help [5]
42. black [8]			

Note: The superscript numbers indicate the *Spelling Plus* list for each word.

SPELLING LIST 4

Name _____

1. *and*

2. *can*

3. *plan*

4. *hand*

5. *stand*

6. *man*

7. *than*

8. *that*

9. *last*

10. *as*

11. *ask*

12. *had*

13. *has*

14. *was*

15. *a*

List 4   Level B, List 1

Words in Patterns:
— Short **a**, Word Bank p. 138.

Review:
— List 1: **am**, **an**, **at**.

Notes to the Teacher:
— The words on this list are the regular, one-syllable words with short **a** which are used most frequently in the English language.
— Teach **as**, **has** and **was** together. Encourage students to see the similarities in orthography. All three words end with the letter **s** spelling the **z** sound. **Was** is a frequently misspelled word. Use it often in review and dictation.
— Children often cannot hear the difference between **than** and **then**. Pronounce them very carefully in dictation. These words were not differentiated until the 1700s. In Dutch, the word **dan**, from the same root, still has both meanings.

Extending the Lesson:
— Dictate regular words with short **a** that are not on this list. A long list of such words is in the Word Bank, p. 138. Do not dictate words ending in **-ck**, **-ll**, **-ff**, **-ss** or **-ve** at this time.

List 5

Level B, List 2

Words in Patterns:
— Short **e**, Word Bank p. 139.

Homophones:
— No homophones need to be taught at this time. Instead, inform students that there are different spellings for some words depending on the meaning, and possibly list **read** on a wall chart for student reference.
— **red / read**
   led / lead

Notes to the Teacher:
— The words on this list are the regular, one-syllable words with short **e** used most frequently in the English language.
— Children sometimes say and write **whent** rather than **went**. This word is often misspelled even by high school students and should be used frequently as a review word and in dictation.
— Many children cannot hear the difference between **then** and **than**. Pronounce these words carefully and show the connection between **then** and **when**. Both end with **en** and both refer to *time*.

Extending the Lesson:
— Dictate regular words with short **e** that are not on this base list. A long list is provided on p. 139. Do not dictate words ending in **-ck**, **-ll**, **-ff**, **-ss** or **-ve** at this time.
— When students are ready, mix in words containing short **a** from the previous list

Name

1. let
2. get
3. yes
4. red
5. led
6. men
7. end
8. went
9. then
10. them
11. best
12. felt
13. help
14. next
15. kept

SPELLING LIST 6

Name

1. is

2. his

3. him

4. big

5. did

6. win

7. sit

8. quit

9. wish

10. with

11. list

12. this

13. the

14. they

15. are

List 6   Level B, List 3

Words in Patterns:
— Short **i**, Word Bank p. 140.
Rule: q is always followed by u in English words.

Review:
— List 2: **if, in, it.**

Notes to the Teacher:
— The words on this list are the regular, one-syllable words with short **i** used most frequently in the English language.
— **Is** and **his.** Remember **as** and **was** also have the **z** sound at the end.
— **Quit** is confused by older students with **quite.** Use this word frequently in review and dictation.
— **Wish** and **with.** Students may say and hear a **wh** at the beginning of these words. These words are frequently misspelled throughout the grades.
— **The** and **they. They** starts with **the.** Teach the two together so they arc linked in students' minds.
— **Are** is irregular. It must be memorized.

Extending the Lesson:
— Dictate regular words with short **i** that are not on this base list. An extended list is provided in the Word Bank, p. 140. Do not dictate words ending in **-ck, -ll, -ff, -ss** or **-ve** at this time.
— When students are ready, mix in words containing short **a** and short **e**, from the previous lists or the Word Bank.

List 7

Level B, List 4

SPELLING LIST 7

Name

Words in Patterns:
— Short **o**, Word Bank p. 141.
— Short **u**, Word Bank p. 142.

Review:
— List 3: **on**, **not**, **got**.

Notes to the Teacher:
— The words on this list are the most frequently used regular one-syllable words containing short **o** and short **u.**
— **A lot** is frequently misspelled as **alot**. **A lot** is taught again as two words on List 52, but dictating **a dog, a lot, a drop**, etc., might prevent students from ever combining the two words.
— **Much** and **such** are the only one-syllable rhyming words spelled with **-uch**. You may wish to write **touch** on a wall chart for student reference. Other rhyming words are spelled with **-tch** as in **clutch**, **crutch** and **Dutch**.
— The short **u** sounds like the schwa sound, which can be spelled with almost any vowel or combination of vowels in an unaccented syllable. In one-syllable words, **u** is most commonly used.

Extending the Lesson:
— Dictate regular words with short **o** and short **u** which are not on this base list. A long list is provided in the Word Bank, pp. 141–142. Do not dictate words ending in **-ck**, **-ll**, **-ff**, **-ss** or **-ve** at this time.
— When students are ready, mix in words containing short **a**, short **e**, and short **i** from previous lists or the Word Bank. Continue throughout the year to dictate mixed sets of words containing short vowels.

1. hot
2. lot
3. dog
4. cost
5. stop
6. drop
7. us
8. up
9. but
10. cut
11. run
12. just
13. must
14. much
15. such

SPELLING LIST 8

Name

1. back
2. black
3. check
4. sick
5. clock
6. luck
7. quick
8. off
9. class
10. pass
11. less
12. miss
13. you
14. your
15. our

List 8   Level B, List 5

Words in Patterns:
— Short vowels in one-syllable words ending in **-ck**, **-ff**, and **-ss**, Word Bank pp. 138–142.

Homophones:
— The difference between **our** and **are** should be taught at this point. They are not technically homophones but are frequently confused.
— Mention that there are different spellings for these words depending on meaning.
  your / **you're**
  our / **are** / **hour**

Notes to the Teacher:
— One-syllable words ending with the sound of **k** end in **-ck**. This was once true for longer words as well, but the **k** has been dropped from **music**, **public**, etc.
— One-syllable words ending with the sound of **f** frequently end with **-ff**. **If** is an exception and was taught on List 2. There are many irregular spellings of this sound: **half**, **calf**, **cough**, **rough**, **tough**, **laugh**, and **deaf**. List irregular words students need for writing on a wall chart.
— One-syllable words ending with the sound of **s** generally end with **-ss**. **Yes** is an exception, as is **gas**, **this**, **bus**, and **plus**. **Guess** has a silent letter.
— **You, your, our.** Notice the **you** in **your** and the **our** in **your**. **Your** and **our** show possession.

Extending the Lesson:
— Mix dictation of any words with short vowels except those ending in **-ll** or **-ve**.

List 9

Level B, List 6

Words in Patterns:

— Regular, one-syllable words ending in **-ll**, Word Bank pp. 139–142.
— Regular, one-syllable words ending in **-ve**, Word Bank p. 142.

Rule: *English words do not end with the letter v.*

Notes to the Teacher:

— The words on this list are the most frequently used English words ending with **-ll** and **-ve**.
— Most one-syllable words ending with the sound of **l** spell it as **-ll**. An exception is words with the short **a** sound, such as **Al**, **gal**, **pal** and **Hal**. With two **l**'s, these words would be **all**, **gall**, **pall** and **hall**. The sound of the **a** would not be short. Point out that the **a** in **all** and other words on this list is not a short **a**.
— Regardless of whether the vowel is long or short, English words do not end with the letter **v**. They end with **-ve**.

Extending the Lesson:

— Mix dictation of any words with short vowels from the Word Bank, pp. 138–142. Continue to do this throughout the year, mixing in words with long vowel sounds later on. One of the most difficult problems in English spelling is knowing when to use double consonants. A thorough knowledge of how to spell regular words with short and long vowel sounds is an excellent foundation for learning when to double consonants before adding a suffix.

Name

1. all
2. call
3. small
4. well
5. tell
6. fill
7. will
8. still
9. full
10. have
11. gave
12. give
13. live
14. five
15. move

SPELLING LIST 10

Name

1. go

2. no

3. so

4. do

5. to

6. be

7. he

8. me

9. we

10. she

11. by

12. my

13. try

14. cry

15. fly

List 10   Level B, List 7

Words in Patterns:
— Words ending in long vowel sounds. Word Bank page numbers are listed below.

Homophones:
— None of these homophones need be taught at this time. Inform students that different spellings for these words exist depending on meaning.
— **so / sow**
  do / dew / due
  to / too / two
  be / bee
  we / wee
  by / buy

Notes to the Teacher:
— **Go**, **no**, **so** are the only common one-syllable words ending with a long **o** spelled as **-o**. The sound is more commonly spelled **-ow** as in **blow**, or **-oe** as in **toe**. Words in these other patterns will be taught later but some may be listed now on a wall chart if students need them for writing. See Word Bank p. 146.
— **Do**, **to**, and **who** are the only one-syllable words ending in this vowel sound spelled as **-o**. The sound is commonly spelled **-ew** as in **chew**, **-ue** as in **true** or **-oo** as in **goo**. Some irregular spellings are **you** and **through**. See Word Bank p. 150.
— **Be**, **he**, **me**, **we** and **she** are the only common one-syllable words in this pattern. The sound is more commonly spelled **-ee** as in **free** or **-ea** as in **tea**. It may also be spelled **-ey** as in **key**. See Word Bank p. 144.
— **By**, **my**, **try**, **cry**, and **fly** are spelled according to the most common pattern. The sound may also be spelled **-ie** as in **die**, **-uy** as in **guy** or **-ye** as in **dye**. See Word Bank p. 145.

Name

List 11   **Level B, List 8**

Words in Patterns:
— Long **a** as in **take**, Word Bank p. 143.

Homophones:
— No homophones need be taught at this time. Mention that these words may be spelled differently depending on meaning.
— **ate / eight**
  made / maid
  sale / sail

Notes to the Teacher:
— The most regular spelling of long **a** is vowel-consonant-silent **e** (v-c-e). Another common spelling is **ai** as in **wait**.

Extending the Lesson:
— Dictate additional words in this pattern. Do not dictate words spelled with **ai** at this time.
— When students are ready, mix dictation of regularly spelled one-syllable words with long **a** and short **a**.
— Regular pluralization of nouns may be introduced at this time: one ___(**name**), two ___(**names**). Add **-s** to the following words from this list: **name, game, state, page, grade, sale, face, place**. Dictate the plural form of these review words: **back, check, clock, dog, drop, list, hand**. Be careful not to dictate any words requiring an **-es** or a change in the base word. Begin using plurals frequently in dictation.

1. came
2. same
3. name
4. game
5. ate
6. state
7. age
8. page
9. take
10. make
11. made
12. grade
13. sale
14. face
15. place

Name

1. time

2. nine

3. line

4. shine

5. nice

6. price

7. life

8. quite

9. like

10. mile

11. smile

12. fire

13. wide

14. side

15. size

List 12 Level B, List 9

Words in Patterns:
— Long **i** as in **nice**, Word Bank p. 145.

Notes to the Teacher:
— The most regular spelling of base words with long **i** is vowel-consonant-silent **e** (v-c-e).
— Students often have difficulty later on spelling such words as **cried** and **cries** where **y** is changed to **i** and **-es** or **-ed** is added. They may spell them according to this pattern as **crise** or **cride**. The rules for adding endings to these words will be taught on List 47. List such words as **cried**, **died**, **dried**, **fried** and **tried** on a wall chart as your students need them in writing.
— Students frequently confuse **quit** and **quite**. Use both words frequently in dictation.
— **-ite** is generally spelled **-ight**. The **gh** was once pronounced as a guttural sound like that in the Scottish **loch**. In fact, at one time **quite** was spelled **quight** and **white** was **whight**. A list of **-ight** words is in the Word Bank on p. 145. You may wish to write any words your students use often in writing on a wall chart.
— Other spellings of the long **i** sound include **climb**, **type** and **rhyme**.

Extending the Lesson:
— Dictate additional words in this pattern.
— When students are ready, mix dictation of long and short **i**, then add words with long and short **a**.
— Pluralize the nouns: one ___(**time**), two ___(**times**). Don't pluralize the word **life**.
— Add **-s** to inflect verbs: they ___(**like**), she ___(**likes**). Verbs from this list: **shine**, **like**, **smile**. Verbs from previous lists: **ask**, **stand**, **plan**, **help**, **get**, **let**, **win**, **sit**, **quit**, **run**, **stop**, **cost**, **tell**, **move**, **live**, **give**, **fill**, and **call**.

List 13

Level B, List 10

Words in Patterns:
— Long **a** at the end of regular one-syllable words as **-ay**, Word Bank p. 143.

Homophones:
— No homophones need be taught at this time. Mention that the following words may be spelled differently depending on meaning.
— **here / hear**
   there / they're / their

Notes to the Teacher:
— The long **a** sound at the end of one-syllable words is most commonly spelled **-ay**.
— **Gray** is spelled **grey** in England and by some Americans. **Gray** is the preferred American spelling. We still spell **they**.
— **Said** is irregular. Have students link it in their minds with **say** and consider having students overpronounce it in their minds so that it rhymes with **paid**. This word is *very* frequently misspelled and should be reviewed again and again during the year.
— **Were** must be memorized. Note the similarity to **here** and link the two words. Students frequently confuse this word with **where**. Pronounce carefully and possibly write **where** on the wall chart.
— The word **here** is in **there**. Both refer to a place. So does **where** which will be taught later.
— **There** and **these** differ by one letter only.

Extending the Lesson:
— Have students add **-s** to **day**, **pay**, **lay**, **way**, **play**, **stay**, and **say**. Dictate mixed review words from previous lists with the plural or inflectional **-s**. Be careful that only **-s** need be added, not **-es** at this time.

Name

1. day
2. may
3. pay
4. lay
5. way
6. away
7. gray
8. play
9. stay
10. say
11. said
12. were
13. here
14. there
15. these

SPELLING LIST 14

Name

1. home

2. hope

3. note

4. chose

5. close

6. those

7. broke

8. love

9. above

10. some

11. come

12. one

13. done

14. gone

15. use

List 14   Level B, List 11

Words in Patterns:
— Long **o** as in **hope**, Word Bank p. 146.
— **o** spelling short **u** sound as in **love**.
— **u** in one-syllable words with vowel - consonant - silent **e** as in **use**.

Homophones:
— No homophones need be taught at this time. Mention that these words may be spelled differently depending on meaning.
— **some / sum**
  one / won

Notes to the Teacher:
— Vowel - consonant - silent **e** is the regular spelling of long **o** in one-syllable words. Another common spelling is **oa**, causing such homophones as **rode / road**.
— **Love, above, some, come,** and **done** use **o** to spell the vowel sound generally spelled with a **u**. The historical story is that medieval scribes closed the **u** in these words. **From** also spells this sound with an **o**. It is not introduced here to prevent the common misspelling **frome** (as in **come**). Other words in this pattern are **dove, glove,** and **shove**.
— **One** and **done** rhyme and can be linked.
— **Done** and **gone** can be linked.
— The vowel - consonant - silent **e** pattern is not commonly used with **u**.
— **Use** can be pronounced two ways, as in, "I am going to **use** it now," and "What's the **use**?"

Extension:
— Add **-s** to nouns and verbs where possible. Can students tell the difference between nouns and verbs?
  Noun: one ___(**home**), two ___(**homes**).
  Verb: they ___(**love**), he ___(**loves**).
  Many words can be nouns *or* verbs.
— **Broke, gone, chose,** and **done** are not *base* forms of verbs and won't take an **-s**.

Level C Test

The emphasis in Level C is on regular words and compound words. Contractions are taught, as well as adding the endings **-es**, **-ed** and **-ing**.

#	Word	#	Word	#	Word	#	Word
1.	walk [16]	43.	horse [17]	84.	understand [25]	125.	arm [16]
2.	its [22]	44.	sleep [15]	85.	both [20]	126.	whole [23]
3.	free [15]	45.	where [23]	86.	doing [19]	127.	month [20]
4.	stood [18]	46.	morning [18]	87.	himself [25]	128.	oh [17]
5.	two [21]	47.	you're [22]	88.	don't [22]	129.	weren't [22]
6.	or [17]	48.	about [17]	89.	car [16]	130.	called [19]
7.	lose [23]	49.	many [21]	90.	ever [21]	131.	only [24]
8.	trying [19]	50.	meet [15]	91.	whether [23]	132.	art [16]
9.	seem [15]	51.	today [25]	92.	true [18]	133.	from [20]
10.	let's [22]	52.	cold [20]	93.	draw [24]	134.	look [18]
11.	goodbye [18]	53.	ground [17]	94.	mind [20]	135.	could [21]
12.	under [24]	54.	whose [23]	95.	upon [25]	136.	stayed [19]
13.	feeling [19]	55.	talk [16]	96.	hard [16]	137.	who's [23]
14.	short [17]	56.	four [21]	97.	awhile [23]	138.	south [17]
15.	deep [15]	57.	without [25]	98.	second [20]	139.	itself [25]
16.	when [23]	58.	over [24]	99.	hour [17]	140.	saw [24]
17.	evening [18]	59.	her [16]	100.	aren't [22]	141.	been [15]
18.	they're [22]	60.	that's [22]	101.	asked [19]	142.	put [25]
19.	out [17]	61.	see [15]	102.	world [24]	143.	find [20]
20.	any [21]	62.	good [18]	103.	war [16]	144.	playing [19]
21.	street [15]	63.	seven [21]	104.	front [20]	145.	into [25]
22.	cannot [25]	64.	north [17]	105.	took [18]	146.	doesn't [22]
23.	old [20]	65.	what [23]	106.	would [21]	147.	dark [16]
24.	found [17]	66.	being [19]	107.	played [19]	148.	very [21]
25.	became [24]	67.	green [15]	108.	who [23]	149.	while [23]
26.	large [16]	68.	I'm [22]	109.	start [16]	150.	their [18]
27.	once [21]	69.	even [18]	110.	welcome [24]	151.	word [24]
28.	outside [25]	70.	become [24]	111.	fact [24]	152.	child [20]
29.	shall [21]	71.	does [19]	112.	need [15]	153.	maybe [25]
30.	want [16]	72.	house [17]	113.	another [25]	154.	warm [16]
31.	it's [22]	73.	keep [15]	114.	most [20]	155.	more [23]
32.	three [15]	74.	which [23]	115.	going [19]	156.	among [20]
33.	foot [18]	75.	blue [18]	116.	themselves [25]	157.	of [17]
34.	six [21]	76.	can't [22]	117.	didn't [22]	158.	haven't [22]
35.	for [17]	77.	around [17]	118.	far [16]	159.	looked [19]
36.	why [23]	78.	never [21]	119.	every [21]	160.	open [24]
37.	crying [19]	79.	week [15]	120.	white [23]	161.	part [16]
38.	seen [15]	80.	inside [25]	121.	boy [18]	162.	other [20]
39.	I'll [22]	81.	told [20]	122.	work [24]	163.	book [18]
40.	hello [18]	82.	act [24]	123.	kind [20]	164.	should [21]
41.	after [24]	83.	feel [15]	124.	forget [25]	165.	filled [19]
42.	goes [19]						

Note: The superscript numbers indicate the *Spelling Plus* list for each word.

Name

Date

1. free
2. three
3. see
4. seem
5. seen
6. green
7. deep
8. sleep
9. keep
10. street
11. meet
12. week
13. feel
14. need
15. been
16.
17.
18.
19.
20.
21.
22.
23.
24.
25.

List 15

Level C, List 1

Words in Patterns:
— Long **e** spelled **-ee** as in **deep**, Word Bank p. 144.

Review:
— **Be**, **he**, **me**, **we**, and **she** from List 10. Make sure students know these words *very* well to avoid confusion as this new list is taught.

Homophones:
— No homophones need be taught at this time. Mention that the following words may be spelled differently depending on meaning.
— **see / sea**
   seem / seam
   seen / scene
   meet / meat (Teach if desired.)
   week / weak (Teach if desired.)

Notes to the Teacher:
— The most common spelling for long **e** in one-syllable words is **ee**.
— **Been** is irregular. As a memory help, have students look for the **be** in **been** and overpronounce it to rhyme with **seen**. Use this word frequently in review and dictation.

Extension:
— Review adding **-s** to pluralize nouns:
   one ___(**week**), two ___(**weeks**)
   Review adding **-s** to inflect verbs:
   they ___(**feel**), it ___(**feels**)
   Which words from this list fit into the noun pattern? Which fit into the verb pattern? Do any words fit into both patterns?

List 16   **Level C, List 2**

Words in Patterns:
— Words containing **-ar** as in **car**, Word Bank p. 148.

Notes to the Teacher:
— The vast majority of one-syllable words with the sound of **-ar** are spelled with **-ar**. Notable exceptions are **guard** and **heart**.
— **Large** and rhyming words end with silent **e**. Otherwise the **g** would be hard.
— **Talk** and **walk**. The **l** was once pronounced. Have students overpronounce these words, giving the **l** its sound. Other words in this pattern are **chalk** and **stalk**.
— **Want** and other words with **wa-** do not rhyme with similarly spelled words (**pant / want; sad / wad, land / wand, dash / wash**).
— **Her** must be memorized. Most rhyming words end in **-ir** as in **stir** or **-ur** as in **fur**. **Her** was not introduced with **here** because it rhymes with **were** and confusion could result. You may wish to now connect **her** and **here** and use a mnemonic sentence, "**Here** is **her** hat." **Per** is the only other common three-letter word spelled in the same pattern as **her**.

Extension:
— Add **-s** to pluralize nouns or inflect verbs.

Name

Date

1. car
2. far
3. dark
4. hard
5. arm
6. warm
7. war
8. art
9. part
10. start
11. large
12. talk
13. walk
14. want
15. her
16.
17.
18.
19.
20.
21.
22.
23.
24.
25.

SPELLING LIST 17

Name _____

Date _____

1. *or*
2. *for*
3. *north*
4. *short*
5. *horse*
6. *house*
7. *out*
8. *about*
9. *around*
10. *found*
11. *ground*
12. *south*
13. *hour*
14. *oh*
15. *of*
16.
17.
18.
19.
20.
21.
22.
23.
24.
25.

List 17   Level C, List 3

Words in Patterns:
— Words containing **-or** as in **for**, Word Bank p. 148.
— Words containing **-ou** as in **our**, Word Bank p. 150.

Homophones:
— No homophones need be taught at this time. Mention that these words may be spelled differently depending on meaning. Review the confusing pair **are** / **our** which was taught on List 8.
— **for** / **four**
  horse / **hoarse**
  hour / **our**

Notes to the Teacher:
— **Or**, **for**, and **nor** are the only one-syllable words ending with the **-or** sound spelled in this pattern.
  More and related words are on List 23.
  Your was taught on List 8.
  Four will be taught on List 21.
  Poor and related words are on List 53.
— Another common spelling for the **ou** sound is **ow**, which is the most common spelling in words rhyming with **growl** and **down**. **Ow** may be used at the end of a word, **ou** is *never* used at the end of a word to spell this sound.
— A word pronounced with **ou** but spelled irregularly is **doubt**. Words spelled with **ou** but pronounced differently are **touch**, **soup**, **group**, and **pour**.
— **Hour** has a silent **h**. Have students pronounce the **h** when spelling this word or use a mnemonic sentence such as, "We spent an **hour** in the **house**."
— **Oh** and **of** are irregular and must be memorized.

List 18

Level C, List 4

Words in Patterns:
— Words with **-oo** as in **took**, Word Bank p. 150.
— Words with **-ue** as in **true**, Word Bank p. 150.
— Words with **-oy** as in **boy**, Word Bank p. 150.

Homophones:
— **there** / **their** Teach at this time.
— **blue** / **blew** Teach if desired. Inform students that there are different spellings for this word depending on the meaning.

Notes to the Teacher:
— **Goodbye** may be spelled **goodbye**, **good-bye**, **goodby**, or **good-by**. Different dictionaries have chosen different preferred spellings. This word is an example of a spelling that has not yet "settled" into a single correct spelling. **Goodbye** was originally a contraction for, "God be with ye."
— Combine **evening** and **morning** with **good** in dictation: Good evening, good morning.
— The most common spelling for **ü** at the end of a word is **-ew**. The spellings of **blue** and **true** are less common. Some other words in this pattern are **clue**, **glue**, **sue**, **due**, and **argue**.
— **Boy** represents a number of words which end in **-oy**. See the Word Bank p. 150 for a complete list.
— **Their** is irregular and must be memorized. It is the #1 most misspelled word by high school students, in part because of confusion with **there** and **they're**. All of these homophones begin with **the**. From this point on, use **their** and **there** frequently in dictation.

Name

Date

1. took
2. look
3. book
4. stood
5. foot
6. good
7. goodbye
8. hello
9. even
10. evening
11. morning
12. blue
13. true
14. boy
15. their
16.
17.
18.
19.
20.
21.
22.
23.
24.
25.

SPELLING LIST 19

Name

Date

1. asked
2. called
3. looked
4. played
5. stayed
6. filled
7. doing
8. going
9. playing
10. trying
11. crying
12. being
13. feeling
14. goes
15. does
16.
17.
18.
19.
20.
21.
22.
23.
24.
25.

List 19   Level C, List 5

Objective:
— Add inflectional endings **-ed**, **-ing**, and **-es** to base words.

Review:
— Review spellings of all base words on this list.

Notes to the Teacher:
— In their writing, your students have likely been using these endings for a long time. Demonstrate adding **-s**, **-ed**, and **-ing** to base words and mention that sometimes **-es** is added instead of **-s**. *Caution:* Do not introduce any words requiring doubling of a final consonant, dropping a silent **e**, or changing **y** to **i** at this time.
— Have students distinctly pronounce two syllables in **doing**, **playing**, **being**, etc. In speech we tend to slur these syllables and misspellings result.
— Children may have trouble hearing the difference between **fill** and **feel**. Pronounce these words distinctly to avoid "hurting someone's fillings."
— **Goes** and **does** must be memorized. Children often write **gose** (rhymes with **those**). Although these two words sound different, they look almost the same. Have students say **go-es** and **do-es** as these words were pronounced centuries ago. Use both words frequently in dictation.
— From this lesson on, have students add these inflectional endings to every spelling word to which they can be added without changes in the base word.

List 20   **Level C, List 6**

Words in Patterns:
— Long vowels in regular one-syllable words, Word Bank pp. 143–146.

Notes to the Teacher:
— The first nine words are regular and easy to spell if the student writes all sounds heard.
— The tenth to fifteenth words are frequently misspelled. Children often add a **u** as in **frount** and **amoung** (rhymes with **young**), or an **e** as in **frome** (rhymes with **come**). Use these words frequently throughout the year in dictation and review.

Extending the Lesson:
— Add **-s** and **-ing** to **find** (**finds**, **finding**) and add **-s** to **month** (**months**).

Name

Date

1. old
2. cold
3. told
4. both
5. most
6. find
7. mind
8. kind
9. child
10. second
11. month
12. among
13. front
14. from
15. other
16.
17.
18.
19.
20.
21.
22.
23.
24.
25.

SPELLING LIST 21

Name _____

Date _____

1. *once*
2. *four*
3. *two*
4. *six*
5. *seven*
6. *any*
7. *many*
8. *never*
9. *ever*
10. *every*
11. *very*
12. *would*
13. *could*
14. *should*
15. *shall*
16.
17.
18.
19.
20.
21.
22.
23.
24.
25.

List 21   Level C, List 7

Words in Patterns:
— Spell numbers.

Review:
— Numbers **one**, **three**, **five**, **nine**, **ten**.

Homophones:
— **four** / **for** Teach this pair now.
— **two** / **to** Teach these now.
— **would** / **wood** Do not teach these now unless there is evidence of confusion.

Notes to the Teacher:
— You may wish to teach the word **eight** with this list. Students are not required to *master* it at this time.
— **Once** is irregular. Note its similarity to **one**. Both words were once pronounced as they are currently spelled.
— **Four** is in the same pattern as **your** and **pour**.
— **Two** is a very irregular spelling. The **w** was once pronounced, as it still is in **twelve**, **twenty** and **twin**.
— **Any** and **many** should be linked in students' minds.
— **Never**, **ever**, and **every** all have the letters **e-v-e-r**.
— **Every** and **very** have the letters **v-e-r-y**.
— **Would**, **could**, and **should** have silent **l**'s which were once pronounced. **Could** once rhymed with **cooled**. Having students overpronounce these words in their minds while spelling them may make it easier to remember the spellings.
— **Shall** does not rhyme with similar words such as **hall**, but rather with words ending in one **l** such as **pal**. Both **shall** and **should** begin with **sh-**.

SPELLING LIST 22

List 22

Level C, List 8

Objective:
— Spell contractions.

Review:
— Spellings of all base words, including **is**, **are**, and **not**.

Homophones:
— **it's** / **its** Teach this pair now.
— **they're** / **there** / **their** Teach these soon.
— **you're** / **your** Teach these now or soon.

Notes to the Teacher:
— Contractions are frequently misspelled in children's writing. Teach students that in a contraction, two words are moved together and an apostrophe replaces the letters left out. The base words *are not changed* except for the apostrophe replacing the letters left out. **Aren't**, **weren't** and **haven't** retain silent **e**'s.
— **Won't** is an irregular contraction for **will not**. It can be linked with **don't**. Dictate it often and ask students what it means.
— Have students form other contractions.

CONTRACTIONS	*I would - I'd*
Contractions are formed with nouns or pronouns and auxiliary verbs or verbs which express a state of being or having.	*you would - you'd* *he would - he'd* *she would - she'd* *it would - it'd* *we would - we'd* *they would - they'd*

I am - I'm *you are - you're* *he is - he's* *she is - she's* *it is - it's* *we are - we're* *they are - they're*	*I will - I'll* *you will - you'll* *he will - he'll* *she will - she'll* *it will - it'll* *we will - we'll* *they will - they'll*	*is not - isn't* *are not - aren't* *was not - wasn't* *were not - weren't* *will not - won't* *would not - wouldn't* *can not - can't* *could not - couldn't* *should not - shouldn't* *has not - hasn't*
I have - I've *you have - you've* *he has - he's* *she has - she's* *it has - it's* *we have - we've* *they have - they've*	*I had - I'd* *you had - you'd* *he had - he'd* *she had - she'd* *it had - it'd* *we had - we'd* *they had - they'd*	*have not - haven't* *had not - hadn't* *does not - doesn't* *do not - don't* *did not - didn't*

Name

Date

1. *its*
2. *it's*
3. *that's*
4. *let's*
5. *I'll*
6. *I'm*
7. *they're*
8. *you're*
9. *can't*
10. *don't*
11. *didn't*
12. *doesn't*
13. *aren't*
14. *weren't*
15. *haven't*
16.
17.
18.
19.
20.
21.
22.
23.
24.
25.

SPELLING LIST 23

Name

Date

1. who
2. who's
3. whose
4. lose
5. why
6. what
7. when
8. where
9. which
10. whether
11. white
12. while
13. awhile
14. whole
15. more
16.
17.
18.
19.
20.
21.
22.
23.
24.
25.

List 23   Level C, List 9

Words in Patterns:
— Words with **wh**.
— Words with **-ore** as in **more**, Word Bank p. 148.

Homophones:
— **who's** / **whose** Teach this pair now.
— **which** / **witch** Mention that **which** is *not* a person or spirit but do not teach this pair until students have mastered **which** because of potential confusion (**wich**, **whitch**).
— **whether** / **weather** Mention that **whether** does *not* refer to climate but do not teach this pair until students have mastered **whether** to avoid confusion (**wheather**, **wether**).
— **whole** / **hole** Teach if confusion exists.

Notes to the Teacher:
— Many students pronounce **w** and **wh** identically, resulting in misspelling of these words. Have students aspirate the **wh** as a memory aid. In Old English, these words were spelled with **hw** rather than **wh** (**hwo** for **who**).
— **Who's** is a contraction of **who is** while **whose** indicates possession. Use these words frequently in dictation. A mnemonic is, "**Whose hose** are those?"
— Both **lose** and **whose** are spelled irregularly and can be linked (contrast with **choose**). A possible mnemonic is "**Whose hose** did you **lose**?"
— **Here** is in the word **where** as it is in **there**. All refer to places.
— **Whether** can be remembered as **whether or not**.
— **While** and **awhile** can be linked.
— The **w** in **whole** is silent. Students may sound it as an aid to memory.
— **More** must be memorized. See Word Bank p. 148 for other words in this pattern.

List 24   Level C, List 10

Words in Patterns:
— Words ending in **-aw** such as **saw**, Word Bank p. 141.
— Words with **wor-** as in **word**, Word Bank p. 149.

Review:
— Review words ending in **-ack** and add the ending **-ed** (**pack** / **packed**). See Word Bank p. 138 for base words.

Notes to the Teacher:
— Most words that rhyme with **act** and **fact** are past tense. Point out that **act** and **fact** are base words and add inflectional endings to them (**act, acts, acted, acting** and **fact, facts**). Be careful that students don't begin spelling rhyming past tense words in this pattern. Mix review in the weeks ahead, for example: "He likes to **act** funny." "She **backed** up."
— **-aw** is the most common spelling for words rhyming with **saw**. Exceptions are **ma** and **pa**.
— **W** can change the pronunciation of a vowel that follows it (**pant** / **want**, **stand** / **wand**, **dash** / **wash**). The only time **-or** has the **ur** sound is when it's preceded by **w**. Words in this pattern include **worm**, **worth**, **worst**, and **worry**. A possible mnemonic sentence is, "The **worst word** in the **world** is **work**."
— **Over**, **under** and **after** end in **-er**. This is the most common spelling for this sound at the end of a word. **-or** is used in some words such as **motor**.
— **Become** and **became** can be taught as combinations of **be + come** and **be + came**. **Welcome**, however, is not **well + come** as it is often misspelled.

1. act
2. fact
3. saw
4. draw
5. work
6. word
7. world
8. only
9. open
10. over
11. under
12. after
13. become
14. became
15. welcome
16.
17.
18.
19.
20.
21.
22.
23.
24.
25.

SPELLING LIST 25

Name _____

Date _____

1. *itself*
2. *himself*
3. *themselves*
4. *into*
5. *upon*
6. *forget*
7. *maybe*
8. *cannot*
9. *today*
10. *inside*
11. *outside*
12. *without*
13. *understand*
14. *another*
15. *put*
16. _____
17. _____
18. _____
19. _____
20. _____
21. _____
22. _____
23. _____
24. _____
25. _____

List 25   Level C, List 11

Objective:
— Spell compound words.
— Pluralize, changing **self** to **selves**.
Guideline: To pluralize many nouns ending with a single *f* or *fe*, change the *f* to *v* and add *-es*. Check the dictionary if in doubt.

Notes to the Teacher:
— Talk about **self** and its irregular plural **selves**. Have students say **themselfs** over and over and try to hear how the f begins to sound like **v**. Remember that **v** is always followed by **e** at the end of a word. Other words with this irregular way of forming plurals include **life**, **wife**, **knife**, **elf**, **shelf**, **calf**, **half**, **wolf**, **leaf**, **loaf**, **thief**, and **scarf**.
— **Itself** and **himself**. The word **self** has not previously been taught. It is not commonly used by children except in compounds, and a common misspelling is to write two words instead of a compound, such as **it self**. Use all related words in dictation, including **herself**, **yourself**, **myself** and **ourselves**.
— Show how two words combine to make one. **Maybe** is a spelling demon for many children. Use it frequently in dictation.
— **Put** is irregular and must be memorized. Other words spelled in the pattern rhyme with **cut**.

Level D Test

The emphasis in Level D is on spelling words with blends and digraphs, and learning to add endings when the base word must be changed by doubling a final consonant or dropping a silent **e**.

1. eat [27]
2. lie [33]
3. smooth [30]
4. along [26]
5. gotten [34]
6. tired [36]
7. first [29]
8. rain [32]
9. east [27]
10. hopping [35]
11. strong [26]
12. piece [33]
13. choose [30]
14. care [28]
15. paid [32]
16. follow [31]
17. leave [27]
18. sudden [34]
19. bring [26]
20. liked [36]
21. too [30]
22. suppose [34]
23. copy [30]
24. sea [28]
25. break [34]
26. low [31]
27. wait [32]
28. better [34]
29. sledding [35]
30. cheat [27]
31. believe [33]
32. school [30]
33. long [26]
34. dinner [34]
35. scared [36]
36. begin [29]
37. plain [32]
38. least [27]
39. getting [35]
40. strength [26]
41. field [33]
42. eye [30]

43. scare [28]
44. laid [32]
45. yellow [31]
46. real [27]
47. happen [34]
48. thing [26]
49. lived [36]
50. loose [30]
51. supposed to [34]
52. wear [30]
53. season [28]
54. third [29]
55. below [31]
56. waiting [32]
57. matter [34]
58. beginning [35]
59. easy [27]
60. pie [33]
61. afternoon [30]
62. length [26]
63. summer [34]
64. swimming [35]
65. began [29]
66. main [32]
67. please [27]
68. running [35]
69. spring [26]
70. chief [33]
71. body [30]
72. animal [28]
73. fail [32]
74. window [31]
75. really [27]
76. happened [34]
77. think [26]
78. used to [36]
79. food [30]
80. bottom [34]
81. bear [30]
82. thank you [26]
83. own [31]

84. die [33]
85. lead [28]
86. stepped [35]
87. using [36]
88. now [29]
89. taking [36]
90. show [31]
91. hear [26]
92. new [33]
93. down [29]
94. again [32]
95. team [28]
96. planned [35]
97. moon [30]
98. giving [36]
99. weak [27]
100. dropping [35]
101. slow [31]
102. read [28]
103. air [32]
104. allow [29]
105. blew [33]
106. reach [27]
107. coming [36]
108. bird [29]
109. raise [32]
110. breakfast [34]
111. year [26]
112. know [31]
113. died [33]
114. leader [28]
115. slipped [35]
116. shining [36]
117. how [29]
118. making [36]
119. shown [31]
120. dear [26]
121. knew [33]
122. brown [29]
123. against [32]
124. mean [28]

125. planning [35]
126. soon [30]
127. living [36]
128. speak [27]
129. stopped [35]
130. grow [31]
131. ready [28]
132. fair [32]
133. power [29]
134. threw [33]
135. teach [27]
136. heart [33]
137. girl [29]
138. reason [28]
139. quiet [34]
140. near [26]
141. known [31]
142. great [34]
143. clean [28]
144. grabbed [35]
145. dining [36]
146. however [29]
147. moving [36]
148. blow [31]
149. clear [26]
150. few [33]
151. town [29]
152. afraid [32]
153. meant [28]
154. dropped [35]
155. room [30]
156. hoping [36]
157. each [27]
158. stopping [35]
159. throw [31]
160. case [28]
161. hair [32]
162. dirty [29]
163. view [33]
164. teacher [27]
165. tomorrow [31]

Note: The superscript numbers indicate the *Spelling Plus* list for each word.

Name

Date

1. along
2. long
3. length
4. strong
5. strength
6. spring
7. bring
8. thing
9. think
10. thank you
11. year
12. near
13. hear
14. dear
15. clear
16.
17.
18.
19.
20.
21.
22.
23.
24.
25.

List 26 Level D, List 1

Words in Patterns:
— Words with **-ng** and **-nk** as in **thing** and **think**, Word Bank p. 147.
— Words with **-ear** as in **year**, Word Bank p. 149.

Homophones:
— **hear** / **here** Teach at this time.
— **dear** / **deer** Teach if there is evidence of confusion.

Notes to the Teacher:
— Have students listen to and write the sounds in **-ang**, **-eng**, **-ing**, **-ong** and **-ung** as well as in **-ank**, **-ink**, **-onk** and **-unk**. Careful pronunciation of words with these sounds may prevent some misspellings such as **thenk**.
— **Long** and **along** should be linked.
— Although **length** and **strength** may not be commonly used at this level, they're frequently misspelled words best taught with **long** and **strong**. There are few common words spelled with **-eng** or **-enk**.
— **Thank you** is taught as two words here because some children tend to combine them (**thankyou**). Teachers may delete the word **you** if they wish.
— You **hear** with your **ear**. **Ear** is not on this list but can be taught and used in dictation.
— Many one-syllable words with the **ear** sound heard in **near** end in **-eer** (**cheer**, **steer**). Students must memorize which is which. Only **here** is spelled with **-ere**. The letters **ear** can also spell the sounds in **wear** and **earth**.

List 27
Level D, List 2

Words in Patterns:
— Long **e** spelled **ea** as in **weak**, Word Bank p. 144.
— Add **-ly** to base words.

Homophones:
— **weak** / **week** Teach at this time.
— **real** / **reel** Teach only if there is evidence of confusion.

Notes to the Teacher:
— The long **e** sound is frequently spelled with either **ee** or **ea**. This causes many homophones (**creak** / **creek**, **read** / **reed**, **steal** / **steel**, etc.). Children must memorize which words are spelled which way.
— Although the teacher should be cautious about introducing homophones that students do not seem to confuse in their writing, this is a good time to begin systematically teaching those that *are* confused, perhaps using the *Homophones Resource Book* (see pp. 28, 169). Introduce no more than one set at a time and work any that have been taught into dictation sentences. Learning to correctly spell homophones is one of the most difficult things about learning to spell in English. Students must *recognize* words that have two or more possible spellings and *think about* which spelling is needed for the meaning intended, a *difficult* task even for computers. Review throughout elementary school is needed. Teachers must be patient and persistent. Homophones can be difficult but are not impossible to learn.
— **Really** has two **l**'s because it is **real + ly**. Add **-ly** directly to base words such as **hot**, **cost**, **sick**, **quick**, **name**, **nice**, **like**, **love**, **free**, **deep**, **week**, **dark**, **hard**, **part**, **large**, **short**, **hour**, **most**, **month**, **open**, **clear**, **near**, **year**, **close**, **wide**, **strong**, **bad**, and **free**. Don't change base words.

Name _____

Date _____

1. *weak*
2. *speak*
3. *each*
4. *reach*
5. *teach*
6. *teacher*
7. *eat*
8. *cheat*
9. *easy*
10. *east*
11. *least*
12. *please*
13. *leave*
14. *real*
15. *really*
16.
17.
18.
19.
20.
21.
22.
23.
24.
25.

SPELLING LIST 28

Name

Date

1. sea
2. season
3. reason
4. lead
5. leader
6. clean
7. team
8. mean
9. meant
10. read
11. ready
12. case
13. care
14. scare
15. animal
16.
17.
18.
19.
20.
21.
22.
23.
24.
25.

List 28   Level D, List 3

Words in Patterns:
— Words with **ea** as in **team**, Word Bank p. 144.
— Words with **-ase** as in **case**, Word Bank p. 143.
— Words with **-are** as in **care**, Word Bank p. 148.

Homophones:
— **sea / see** Teach if there is evidence of confusion.

Notes to the Teacher:
— **-ea** may spell either the short or long **e** sound. Rarely, it spells long **a** as in **great**. Many words using **ea** for the short sound are on List 39. **Meant** and **ready** are on this list because of the link to **mean** and **read**.
— **Season** and **reason** should be linked. *Caution:* Some students may generalize and write **beacause**. Although **because** need not be *mastered* until List 41, it is frequently used and may be taught as early as List 24. Have it on a wall chart or teach it as a personal word.
— **Lead** and **read** may be pronounced with either a short **e** or long **e** sound.
— **Meant** and **ready** are frequently misspelled **ment** and **reddy**, spellings more sensible, perhaps, than the correct ones. Have children say **mean - t** and link **read** and **ready**. Use both words frequently in dictation.
— A more common spelling for words rhyming with **case** is with **-ace** as in **face**.
— The sound for **-are** in **care** may be spelled as in **pear**, **pare** or **pair**. This causes many homophones. The most common spelling is **-are**. Memorization is necessary.

List 29　　Level D, List 4

Words in Patterns:
— **-ow** as in **down**, Word Bank p. 150.
— **-ir** as in **bird**, Word Bank p. 149.

Review:
— Review spellings of **ever**, **other**, **whether**, **over**, **under**, **after**, **teacher**, and **leader**. Note **-er** is common at the *end* of a word.

Notes to the Teacher:
— The **ow** sound can be spelled with either **ow** or **ou** (see List 17). **Ou** is never used at the end of a word to spell this sound. **Ow** can be used within or at the end of a word.
— With **however**, show **whenever**, **whoever**, **whatever**, **wherever** and **whichever**.
— The **ur** sound can be spelled with **-er**, **-ir**, **-or** (**wor**), **-ur**, **-ear**, or **-our**. Before 1560, each spelling of this sound was pronounced differently. **Bird** was pronounced with the **i** sound in **bid**, and sounded like **beard**. Because of the pronunciation change, this sound is troublesome for spellers. Create mnemonic sentences to group words with each spelling, such as: "**I** saw the **third girl** take the **first dirty bird**."
— **Begin** and **began** differ by only one letter and can be linked. You may wish to talk about irregular past tense verbs at this point. All words listed below have been taught on previous spelling lists.
Today I _____ (begin).
Yesterday I _____ (began).

stand / stood	**give / gave**
has, have / had	**come / came**
get / got	**eat / ate**
go / went	**take / took**
feel / felt	**make / made**
keep / kept	**see / saw**
do / did	**find / found**
sit / sat	**forget / forgot**
run / ran	**become / became**
tell / told	**lead / led**
mean / meant	**read / read**

Name _____

Date _____

1. *now*
2. *how*
3. *however*
4. *down*
5. *brown*
6. *town*
7. *allow*
8. *power*
9. *dirty*
10. *bird*
11. *girl*
12. *third*
13. *first*
14. *begin*
15. *began*
16.
17.
18.
19.
20.
21.
22.
23.
24.
25.

Name _____

Date _____

1. *too*
2. *loose*
3. *food*
4. *moon*
5. *soon*
6. *room*
7. *smooth*
8. *school*
9. *afternoon*
10. *choose*
11. *eye*
12. *body*
13. *copy*
14. *wear*
15. *bear*
16.
17.
18.
19.
20.
21.
22.
23.
24.
25.

List 30   Level D, List 5

Words in Patterns:

— Words with **oo** as in **loose**, Word Bank p. 150.
— Words with **ear** as in **bear**, Word Bank p. 148.

Homophones:

— **too / to / two** Teach now and begin using frequently in dictation.
Teach the following sets of homophones only if there is evidence of confusion.
— **eye / I**
   bear / bare

Notes to the Teacher:

— Review **to** and **two**. Introduce **too** with its meaning. Point out that **too** has **too** many **o**'s. Its other meaning is **also**. **Too** is the second most frequently misspelled word by high school students. From now until the end of sixth grade, **to**, **too** and **two** should be included in dictation sentences at least once or twice every week if students are to master this!

— **Loose** has a soft **s**. **Choose** does not. That is why they are separated on the list. **Lose** was linked with **whose** on List 23. There is a great deal of potential for confusion here. Use all of these words in dictation frequently.

— **Afternoon** is compound, **after + noon**.

— **Body** and **copy** have short vowel sounds which are generally followed by double consonants (**shoddy**, **choppy**). These two words must be memorized.

— **Wear** and **bear** use **ear** to spell the sound heard in **air**. Other words in this pattern are **tear**, **pear** and **swear** (not **prayer**). Be careful that students distinguish between **wear** and **where,** and understand that **where** contains the word **here**. Both refer to place.

List 31   Level D, List 6

Words in Patterns:
— Words with **ow** as in **show**, Word Bank p. 146.

Homophones:
— **know** / **no** Teach now and begin using in dictation.

Review:
— Words spelled with **ow** in List 29.

Notes to the Teacher:
— **Go**, **so**, and **no** are the only common one-syllable words ending with the long **o** sound spelled as **-o** rather than **-ow** (**tow**) or **-oe** (**toe**).
— Until this list, there have been no words introduced with **kn**. Long ago, the **k** was pronounced. Students may pronounce **know** as **k-no**.
— **Own**, **known** and **shown** are similar and can be linked.
— **Below** has a long **e** just before the **l**, hence there is just one **l**. Contrast with **bellow**. **Follow** and **yellow** have short vowels just before the **l**, hence the double consonant.
— **Tomorrow** is a frequently misspelled word (How many **m**'s? How many **r**'s?). Teaching it as **tom - or - row** and having students recall that mnemonic every time it's reviewed or dictated may help. Use this word frequently in dictation.

Extension:
— Have students add **-s** and **-ing** to: **know**, **show**, **blow**, **snow**, **grow**, **throw**, **follow**.
— Add **-ed** to **show**, **snow**, and **follow**.
— Add **-ly** to **slow**.

Name _____

Date _____

1. own
2. know
3. known
4. show
5. shown
6. blow
7. slow
8. grow
9. throw
10. low
11. below
12. follow
13. yellow
14. window
15. tomorrow
16.
17.
18.
19.
20.
21.
22.
23.
24.
25.

SPELLING LIST 32

Name _____

Date _____

1. wait
2. waiting
3. rain
4. plain
5. main
6. paid
7. laid
8. fail
9. again
10. against
11. afraid
12. air
13. fair
14. hair
15. raise
16.
17.
18.
19.
20.
21.
22.
23.
24.
25.

List 32   Level D, List 7

Words in Patterns:
— Words with **ai** as in **wait**, Word Bank p. 143.
— Words with **air** as in **fair**, Word Bank p. 148.

Homophones:
Any of the following homophones may be taught, especially if students confuse them in writing:
— **plain** / **plane**
— **main** / **mane**
— **fair** / **fare**
— **rain** / **rein** / **reign**

Notes to the Teacher:
— Children frequently hear or say **wh** for the **w** in **wait**. Pronounce it carefully, voicing the **w**. **Waiting** is frequently pronounced **wading**.
— **Paid** and **laid** are irregular past tense forms. Normally, in words ending in **-ay**, an **-ed** is added to form past tense, as in **play** / **played**. These two must be memorized as irregular. **Said** (from **say**) is formed the same way but is pronounced differently.
— Pronouncing **again** and **against** with a long **a** sound (British accent) makes it easier to spell these two words, which should be linked.
— **Air**, **fair** and **hair**. Other words in this pattern are **chair**, **pair**, and **stair**.

Extension:
— Have students add **-s**, **-ed**, and **-ing** to **wait**, **rain** and **fail**.
— Have students add **-ly** to **plain**, **main** and **fair**.

List 33   **Level D, List 8**

Words in Patterns:
— Words with **ew** as in **new**, p. 150.
— Words with **ie** as in **pie**, p. 145.
— Words with **ie** as in **grief**, p. 144.
Rule: *Write **i** before **e** except after **c**. See p. 129 for more about this rule.*

Homophones:
The following homophones should be taught, especially if students confuse them in writing:
— **new / knew**
— **blew / blue**
— **piece / peace**
Inform students that these homophones exist and teach if needed:
— **threw / through**
— **die / dye**

Notes to the Teacher:
— The **ew** sound in **new** can also be spelled **ue** (see List 18) and **oo** (see List 30). Learning which word is spelled which way is a matter of memorization.
— **Know**, **knew** and **known** should be linked as related words.
— **Know / knew**, **blow / blew** and **throw / threw** are irregular in the past tense. **Grow / grew** is also in this pattern.
— **Threw / through** can be *very* confusing for students. Write **through** on a wall chart.
— **View** can be overpronounced **vi - ew**.
— **Lie** and **believe** mnemonic: "Don't be**lie**ve a **lie**."
— **Pie** and **piece** mnemonic: "Have a **pie**ce of **pie**." This also helps with meaning. Contrast with **peace**.
— **Field** and **chief**. Other common words in this pattern are **grief** and **thief**.
— **Heart** is very irregular. "Can you **hear** with your **hear**t?"

Name

Date

1. *new*
2. *knew*
3. *few*
4. *blew*
5. *threw*
6. *view*
7. *die*
8. *died*
9. *lie*
10. *believe*
11. *pie*
12. *piece*
13. *field*
14. *chief*
15. *heart*
16.
17.
18.
19.
20.
21.
22.
23.
24.
25.

SPELLING LIST 34

Name

Date

1. better
2. matter
3. gotten
4. dinner
5. summer
6. sudden
7. happen
8. happened
9. suppose
10. supposed to
11. bottom
12. great
13. break
14. breakfast
15. quiet
16.
17.
18.
19.
20.
21.
22.
23.
24.
25.

List 34   Level D, List 9

Words in Patterns:
— Double consonants after short vowels.

Homophones:
The following homophones should be taught, especially if students confuse them in writing:
— **break / brake**
— **quiet / quite** (not homophones but frequently confused)
Inform students that these homophones exist:
— **great / grate**

Notes to the Teacher:
— Point out the short vowels followed by double consonants in the list. *Without* the double consonant, they'd be pronounced with long vowels.
— The word **gotten** was used in England in Shakespeare's time but is now considered by the British to be an Americanism.
— **Happened.** Because the **e** in **-ed** is not pronounced, this word may be misspelled **happend**.
— **Supposed to** is taught as two words. Children may not hear the **d** in **supposed** and therefore write **suppose to**.
— **Bottom. Tom** is at the **bottom**.
— **Great**, **break**, and **steak** are the only common one-syllable words spelling the long **a** sound with **ea**. Link them.
— **Break + fast = breakfast.** To **fast** is to go without food. We **fast** at night when we sleep and in the morning we break the fast by eating **breakfast**. Pronounce it as **break fast** for purposes of spelling.
— **Quiet** is often confused with **quite** or **quit**. Clearly pronounce it with two syllables.

Extension:
— Add **-ly** to **sudden**, **great**, **quiet**.
— Add **-s**, **-ed**, and **-ing** to **happen**.

List 35   **Level D, List 10**

Objective:
— Double final consonant and add **-ed**, **-ing**.
Rule: *When a one-syllable word ends with a short vowel and a single consonant, double the final consonant before adding a suffix beginning with a vowel. In a two-syllable word such as* **begin**, *this rule applies when the accent is on the last syllable.*

Review:
Spend a good deal of time dictating words such as **hop / hope**, **cut / cute**, etc. before introducing this list. See Word Bank p. 147. Students who *recognize* short and long vowel sounds and can spell the base words easily will have much less trouble with this concept.

Notes to the Teacher:
— Dictate all base words, then teach and model the rule and have students add the endings. For example:
step + ed = stepped
run + ing = running
Note that this rule only applies to suffixes beginning with a *vowel*. It does not apply to the endings **-s** or **-ly**.
— The words on this list are among the most misspelled words in English! Teach and reteach, review and re-review. Dictate *any* appropriate words with short vowel sounds (Word Bank pp. 138–142) except those ending with two consonants (**back**, **puff**, **kill** or **pass**). Have students apply the rule to add **-ed** and **-ing**.
— **Beginning** is 17th on the list of words most frequently misspelled by high school students. The **n** is doubled because the accent is on the *last* syllable.
Opening does not double the **n** because the accent is on the *first* syllable.
Penning would double the consonant.
— Students should master this rule before the next list is introduced.

Name _____

Date _____

1. stepped
2. slipped
3. grabbed
4. planned
5. planning
6. dropped
7. dropping
8. stopped
9. stopping
10. hopping
11. getting
12. running
13. sledding
14. swimming
15. beginning
16.
17.
18.
19.
20.
21.
22.
23.
24.
25.

Name

Date

1. tired
2. scared
3. liked
4. lived
5. used to
6. using
7. shining
8. dining
9. taking
10. making
11. moving
12. giving
13. living
14. hoping
15. coming
16.
17.
18.
19.
20.
21.
22.
23.
24.
25.

List 36   Level D, List 11

Objective:
— Drop silent **e** and add **-ed**, **-ing**.
Rule: *When a word ends in silent **e**, drop the e before adding a suffix beginning with a vowel. Keep the silent e before a suffix beginning with a consonant.*

Caution:
Before introducing this list, make sure students are *very* competent with the rule introduced on List 35. Spend time reviewing words in the regular **c-v-c-e** pattern (consonant - vowel - consonant - silent **e**). Examples are in the Word Bank pp. 143–147. Dictate pairs such as **hop** / **hope**, **cut** / **cute**. Students who have mastered the spellings of regular base words will be well prepared.

Notes to the Teacher:
— Dictate all base words, then teach and model the rule and have students add the endings. For example:
  tire + ed = tired
  shine + ing = shining
  Note that this rule only applies to suffixes beginning with a *vowel*. It does not apply to the endings **-s** or **-ly**.
— Technically, in a word like **scare**, the silent **e** is dropped and **-ed** is added. Students may think they're just adding a **d** which could cause mistakes with other words such as **learnd** and **happend**.
— **Used to** is included as two words because it's often misspelled as **use to**.
— Contrast **dining**, **diner** and **dinner**. Notice the short and long vowel sounds.
— Review words utilizing the two rules introduced in the last two lessons *hundreds* even *thousands* of times. Include them in dictation almost daily. If students leave the third grade able to spell words like **hopping** and **hoping** correctly every time, they'll have made great progress toward learning to spell well!

Level E Test

The emphasis in Level E is on commonly used words with unusual or difficult spellings, and on changing **y** to **i** before adding a suffix.

1. fight [40]
2. Sunday [43]
3. bought [41]
4. nobody [37]
5. carry [45]
6. laughter [42]
7. cover [38]
8. across [46]
9. search [39]
10. happiness [47]
11. night [40]
12. anybody [37]
13. Wednesday [43]
14. though [41]
15. pretty [45]
16. corner [38]
17. address [46]
18. everywhere [37]
19. taught [42]
20. earth [39]
21. between [41]
22. program [44]
23. high [40]
24. Saturday [43]
25. always [46]
26. buy [40]
27. (your city) [40]
28. circle [44]
29. surprise [44]
30. light [40]
31. Monday [43]
32. brought [41]
33. nothing [37]
34. hurry [45]
35. caught [42]
36. later [38]
37. unless [46]
38. heard [39]
39. business [47]
40. right [40]
41. everyone [37]
42. Thursday [43]
43. through [41]
44. family [45]
45. water [38]
46. lesson [46]
47. somebody [37]
48. course [42]
49. learn [39]
50. private [41]
51. problem [44]
52. Mr. [40]
53. hurt [43]
54. pleasant [39]
55. middle [44]
56. (your state) [40]
57. single [44]
58. surprised [44]
59. might [40]
60. Tuesday [43]
61. thought [41]
62. anyway [37]
63. happy [45]
64. laughed [42]
65. center [38]
66. recess [46]
67. early [39]
68. beautiful [47]
69. tight [40]
70. everything [37]
71. Friday [43]
72. enough [41]
73. beauty [45]
74. winter [38]
75. carrying [46]
76. something [37]
77. fourth [42]
78. learned [39]
79. friend [41]
80. promise [44]
81. Ms. [40]
82. somewhere [37]
83. busy [45]
84. write [42]
85. studied [47]
86. wonder [38]
87. carried [47]
88. people [44]
89. weather [39]
90. enemy [45]
91. return [43]
92. America [40]
93. handwriting [42]
94. stories [47]
95. watch [37]
96. hurrying [46]
97. tough [41]
98. cries [47]
99. awful [38]
100. although [46]
101. wreck [42]
102. head [39]
103. trouble [44]
104. group [41]
105. lucky [45]
106. further [43]
107. type [38]
108. death [39]
109. important [44]
110. almost [46]
111. sometimes [37]
112. city [45]
113. writer [42]
114. prettier [47]
115. wonderful [38]
116. easiest [47]
117. chocolate [44]
118. measure [39]
119. hungry [45]
120. during [43]
121. American [40]
122. wrote [42]
123. tried [47]
124. stretch [37]
125. studying [46]
126. touch [41]
127. countries [47]
128. until [38]
129. alone [46]
130. written [42]
131. bread [39]
132. terrible [44]
133. before [41]
134. study [45]
135. sure [43]
136. road [38]
137. instead [39]
138. turn [43]
139. already [46]
140. catch [37]
141. story [45]
142. writing [42]
143. earlier [47]
144. careful [38]
145. luckily [47]
146. favorite [44]
147. heavy [39]
148. country [45]
149. purpose [43]
150. United States [40]
151. wrong [42]
152. hurried [47]
153. little [37]
154. student [46]
155. young [41]
156. families [47]
157. yesterday [38]
158. lonely [46]
159. laugh [42]
160. dead [39]
161. remember [44]
162. because [41]
163. sorry [45]
164. sugar [43]
165. board [38]

Note: The superscript numbers indicate the *Spelling Plus* list for each word.

Name

Date

1. *nobody*
2. *nothing*
3. *anyway*
4. *anybody*
5. *everyone*
6. *everything*
7. *everywhere*
8. *somebody*
9. *something*
10. *somewhere*
11. *sometimes*
12. *catch*
13. *watch*
14. *stretch*
15. *little*
16.
17.
18.
19.
20.
21.
22.
23.
24.
25.

List 37   Level E, List 1

Words in Patterns:
— Compound words.
— Words ending with **-tch** as in **watch**, Word Bank pp. 138–142.
Guideline: Add -es rather than -s to words ending with the sound of s, x, z, sh, or ch.

Review:
— Review **much** and **such** from List 7.

Notes to the Teacher:
— The compound words on this list are frequently misspelled as two words. Letters are often left out as in **everthing** or **somone**. Write these two columns on the board and have students come up with as many combinations as they can:

no	**one**
any	**thing**
some	**body**
every	**where**

Caution: **No one** is written as two words because **noone** would not show the correct pronunciation.
— Generally, short vowel sounds followed by the **ch** sound are spelled with **tch**. Students may be able to *feel* a **t** when they say the words. Some common words which do *not* end with **tch** are **much**, **such**, **rich**, **which** and the irregular **touch**. Write these words on a wall chart to avoid possible confusion.
— Add **-es** not **-s** to words ending in the sound of **s**, **x**, **z**, **sh**, or **ch**. **Watch** becomes **watches**. **Stretch** becomes **stretches**.
— As with **pant** and **want**, the **w** changes the vowel sound of **a** in **catch** and **watch**. Link **catch** and **watch** so students don't write **wotch**.
— Notice the two **t**'s after the short **i** in **little**.

List 38 — Level E, List 2

Words in Patterns:
— Two-syllable words ending with **-er**.
— Add the suffix **-ful**.
— Words with **oa** as in **road**, Word Bank p. 146.

Homophones:
The following homophones cause considerable confusion and should be taught:
— **board / bored**
— **road / rode**

Notes to the Teacher:
— The most common way to spell the **ur** sound at the end of a word is with **-er**. Words like **doctor**, **motor**, and **author**, however, do not follow this pattern.
— The suffix **-ful** has only *one* **l**. It forms an adjective or a noun and means *full of, characterized by, or having the qualities of.* Which meaning does it have in each word on the list? Generally, add **-ful** directly without changing the base word.
— Students can add **-ful** to the following words from previous spelling lists to form adjectives:

help	**forget**	**hope**
play	**wish**	**watch**

Consider having them add **-ful** to **hand** and **arm**. These words remain nouns.
— **Awful** is an exception. It doesn't keep its silent **e** (**awe + ful**) according to the rule.
— **Until** has only one **l**.
— **Yesterday** should be pronounced with three distinct syllables: **yes - ter - day**.
— **Type**. Only a very few words use **y** to spell the long **i** sound in the middle of a word. Another is **style**.
— **Board**. "They used a bo**ard** for an o**ar**." **Bored** is **bore + ed**. In it, the silent **e** is dropped and **-ed** is added. **Boring** drops silent **e** and adds **-ing**.
— Possible personal words include: **style**, **boring**, **bored**.

Name _____

Date _____

1. cover
2. later
3. center
4. corner
5. water
6. winter
7. wonder
8. wonderful
9. careful
10. awful
11. until
12. yesterday
13. type
14. road
15. board
16.
17.
18.
19.
20.
21.
22.
23.
24.
25.

SPELLING LIST 39

Name

Date

1. weather
2. measure
3. heavy
4. head
5. bread
6. dead
7. death
8. instead
9. pleasant
10. search
11. heard
12. early
13. earth
14. learn
15. learned
16.
17.
18.
19.
20.
21.
22.
23.
24.
25.

List 39   Level E, List 3

Words in Patterns:
— Words with **ea** as in **head**, Word Bank p. 139.
— Words with **ear** as in **earth**, Word Bank p. 149.

Homophones:
The following homophones cause considerable confusion and should be taught:
— **weather** / **whether**
— **heard** / **herd**

Notes to the Teacher:
— **Weather** and **whether** are often misspelled. The mnemonic **we - at - her** may help, or the mnemonic sentence, "We **eat** in all kinds of we**at**her." Use both **weather** and **whether** frequently in dictation.
— **Please** can be linked with **pleasant**.
— **Ear** can be linked with **hear** and **heard**. "You h**ear**d it with your **ear**."
— Form **learned** from **learn** by adding **-ed**.
— Possible personal words include: **feather**, **leather**, **pleasure**, **treasure**, **spread**, **earn**.

Extension:
— Add **-ing** to **learn** and **search**.
— Add **-ly** to **dead**, **pleasant**, **earth**.

List 40

Level E, List 4

Teachers:
Write the name of your city on line 10 and your state on line 11 before reproducing.

Words in Patterns:
— Words with **-igh** as in **light**, Word Bank p. 145.
Rule: *Capitalize proper nouns.*

Homophones:
The following homophones cause considerable confusion and should be taught:
— **buy / by**
These homophones should be pointed out but need not be taught unless there is evidence of confusion in student writing:
— **high / hi**
— **night / knight**
— **right / rite / write**

Notes to the Teacher:
— *Many* common words are spelled with **-igh** and **-ight**. The **gh** was once pronounced as a guttural sound like that in the Scottish **loch**. The spellings have not been updated. *Caution:* The word **height** is not in this pattern.
— **Mr.** and **Ms.** are seldom written except as abbreviations. Periods show that these are abbreviations. Capitalize titles.
— Proper nouns. Names of places you would find on a map are always capitalized. Your city is one of many cities. Your state is one of many states. The **United States** is one of many countries. Have students give examples.
— **Buy** is an unusual spelling. The only other word in this pattern is **guy**. Use **buy** and **by** frequently in dictation.
— Possible personal words include: **slight**, **slightly**, **Mrs.** and **guy**.

Name

Date

1. *fight*
2. *light*
3. *might*
4. *night*
5. *right*
6. *tight*
7. *high*
8. *Mr.*
9. *Ms.*
10.
11.
12. *America*
13. *American*
14. *United States*
15. *buy*
16.
17.
18.
19.
20.
21.
22.
23.
24.
25.

Name _____

Date _____

1. bought
2. brought
3. thought
4. though
5. through
6. enough
7. tough
8. touch
9. young
10. group
11. before
12. because
13. between
14. private
15. friend
16. _____
17. _____
18. _____
19. _____
20. _____
21. _____
22. _____
23. _____
24. _____
25. _____

List 41   Level E, List 5

Words in Patterns:
— Words with **-ough**.

Homophones:
The following homophones were introduced on List 33. They should be taught to mastery at this time.
— **through / threw**

Notes to the Teacher:
— The first three words on this list are irregular past tense forms: **buy / bought, bring / brought, think / thought.** Another word in this pattern is **fight / fought.**
— There are three sounds for **-ough** in this list. All sounded the same centuries ago. **Ough** is now pronounced in several ways, as in: **tough, though, thought, through, bough, cough,** and **hiccough.**
— **Tough, touch, young** and **group** can be linked, as with the sentence: "Don't **touch** that **tough young group** of cats!" If our spelling was consistent, **touch** would be **tuch** or **tutch, tough** would be **tuff, young** would be **yung** and **group** would be **groop.** Caution students not to generalize and write **frount, mounth** and **secound** for **front, month** and **second.**
— The **fore** in **before** is a combining form also used in **forehead,** *not* the word **for.**
— **Friend** can be remembered as **fri - end** or with the mnemonic: "He's my fri**end** to the **end.**"
— Possible personal words include: **ought, fought, dough, thorough, thoroughly, throughout, rough.**

Extension:
— Have students add suffixes to any of the words to make new words. For example: **touched, friendly, groups, thoughtful, thoughtfully, roughly.**

List 42

Level E, List 6

Words in Patterns:
— Words with **wr**.
— Words with **augh**.
— Words with **our** as in **course**, Word Bank p. 148.

Homophones:
The following homophones cause considerable trouble and should be taught to mastery. Use them frequently in dictation:
— **write / right**
These homophones need not be taught unless there is evidence of confusion, but may be mentioned:
— **wrote / rote**
— **caught / cot**
— **taught / tot**
— **course / coarse**
— **fourth / forth**

Notes to the Teacher:
— The **w** in **wr** was sounded centuries ago. As a memory aid, have students sound the **w** as they **w-rite** these words.
— **Writer** and **writing**: Drop the silent **e** and add the suffix.
— **Handwriting** is a compound word.
— **Written**. Point out the short vowel followed by a double consonant. This word may cause some students a great deal of trouble and should be used frequently in dictation.
— **Laugh** is very irregular and must be memorized. Add **-ed**, **-ter**, and **-ing**.
— **Caught** and **taught** are past tense forms of words ending in **ch**:
  catch / caught   **teach / taught**
  The word **daughter** will be on List 50.
— **Course** and **fourth** can be linked.
— **Fourth** is **four + th**. Add **-th** to other numbers such as **six**, **seven**, **eight** and **ten**. **Fifth** and **ninth** are different.
— Possible personal words include: **wrist**, **wrap**, **fifth**, **ninth**.

Name ___
Date ___

1. write
2. writer
3. writing
4. handwriting
5. wrote
6. wrong
7. wreck
8. written
9. laugh
10. laughed
11. laughter
12. caught
13. taught
14. course
15. fourth
16.
17.
18.
19.
20.
21.
22.
23.
24.
25.

Name

Date

1. Sunday
2. Monday
3. Tuesday
4. Wednesday
5. Thursday
6. Friday
7. Saturday
8. hurt
9. turn
10. return
11. during
12. purpose
13. further
14. sure
15. sugar
16.
17.
18.
19.
20.
21.
22.
23.
24.
25.

List 43 Level E, List 7

Words in Patterns:
— Names of days of the week, capitalized.
— Words with **ur** as in **hurt**, Word Bank p. 149.

Notes to the Teacher:
— Students may be interested in the derivations of our names for the days of the week. The seven-day week comes from the Bible. The Romans named the days after the sun, the moon, and the five planets known at the time, which had been named after Roman gods. The Anglo-Saxons renamed the days after their own Norse gods, as Sun's day, Moon's day, Tiw's day (god of war), Woden's day (chief god), Thor's day (god of thunder), Frigg's day (goddess of love) and Seterne's day (Saturn).
— **Wednesday** can be overpronounced as **Wed - nes - day**.
— **Thursday** and **Saturday** spell the **ur** sound with **ur**.
— The **ur** words may be linked with a mnemonic sentence such as, "He **hurt** me on **purpose during** his **turn**."
— The prefix **re-** added to **turn** means turn *back*. **Re-** can also mean *again*.
— **Sure** and **sugar** are the only common words that use **s** to spell the **sh** sound.

Extension:
— Add **-ly** to **purpose, sure**.
— Add the prefix **re-** to other words that have been taught in previous lists. Does it mean *back* or *again* in each case?

do	name	touch	word
did	take	use	think
check	make	start	teach
call	cover	write	read
tell	sale	mind	copy
fill	place	act	paid
live	pay	draw	new
move	play	work	run

List 44

Level E, List 8

Words in Patterns:
— Words ending in **-le**.
— Words beginning with **pro-**.
Guideline: Few common words end with -ise. With the exception of surprise, exercise, advertise, and revise, common words with this final sound end in -ize.

Review:
Review the word **little**. This was taught on List 37 to hopefully avoid confusion with **middle**.

Notes to the Teacher:
— Overpronounce difficult words to give all written letters their full sound value. Think of these exaggerated pronunciations whenever the words are spelled:
people — pe - o - ple
chocolate — choc - o - late
favorite — fav - o - rite
trouble — tro - u - ble
remember — re - mem - ber
important — im - por - tant
surprise — sur - prise
Give the last **s** a soft sound in **surprise**.
— Does **remember** mean to **member** *back* or *again?* Not really, but the **member** in this word comes from the same root as **memory**. **Remember** means to bring back to memory.
— **Surprise** has the same **ur** spelling as **purpose**.
— Overpronouncing **pro - blem**, and **pro - mise** with a long **o** may help with spelling.
— Suggestions for personal words include: **double, exercise** (on List 59), **advertise, revise, probably** (on List 56), **proper, property, project, provide, pronounce**.

Name _____

Date _____

1. circle
2. single
3. middle
4. people
5. chocolate
6. favorite
7. trouble
8. terrible
9. remember
10. important
11. surprise
12. surprised
13. program
14. problem
15. promise
16.
17.
18.
19.
20.
21.
22.
23.
24.
25.

Name

Date

1. busy
2. city
3. story
4. enemy
5. hungry
6. country
7. lucky
8. study
9. sorry
10. carry
11. hurry
12. happy
13. pretty
14. family
15. beauty
16.
17.
18.
19.
20.
21.
22.
23.
24.
25.

List 45

Level E, List 9

Words in Patterns:
— Words ending in **-y**.

Notes to the Teacher:
— **Busy** is a very irregular spelling. See p. 6 for the historical story. Overpronounce it as **bus - y**.
— There is a **count** in the **country**.
— **Lucky** is **luck** plus the suffix **-y** meaning *full of* or *like*. This suffix may be added to other words which have been taught on previous lists:

hand	**hard**	**might**	**dirt**
class	**room**	**rain**	**hair**
sleep	**show**	**catch**	**sugar**
need	**water**	**winter**	**good**

— Notice the short vowels and double consonants in **happy** and **pretty**. **Sorry**, **carry**, and **hurry** also have double consonants. **Study** does *not* although **muddy** does. **Study** may be pronounced **stoo - dy**, with the same vowel sound as in **student** as an aid to spelling.
— **Family** can be pronounced **fam - i - ly**. **Beauty** can be pronounced **be - a - uty**, or use the mnemonic sentence, "**Be a beau**ty."

List 46   Level E, List 10

Words in Patterns:
— Words beginning with **al-**.
— Words ending in **-ss**.
— Add the suffix **-ly**.
— Add **-ing** to words ending in **y**.

Review:
Review adding **-ly** to **real** and other words. See List 27.

Notes to the Teacher:
— Except for **all right**, many common words begin with **al-** and are written as one word.
— **Lonely** does *not* drop the silent **e** before adding **-ly** because the suffix begins with a consonant. Add **-ly** to more words which have been taught in previous spelling lists:

clean	loose	smooth	plain
main	fair	slow	chief
sudden	great	quiet	careful
awful	dead	light	night
right	tight	high	private
friend	wrong	purpose	sure

Truly is the notable exception.
— **Across** is often misspelled **accross**. Think of **a cross**.
— Add **-ful** and then **-ly** to the following words (**play + ful + ly = playfully**):
play   hope   care   watch
— Add **-ing** directly to words ending in **y**. Pronounce three syllables distinctly:
carrying, say **car - ry - ing**
hurrying, say **hur - ry - ing**
studying, say **stu - dy - ing**
These words are *very* frequently misspelled as **carring**, **hurring**, and **studing**.
— **Study** and **student** should be linked.

Name

Date

1. always
2. almost
3. already
4. although
5. alone
6. lonely
7. across
8. unless
9. recess
10. address
11. lesson
12. carrying
13. hurrying
14. studying
15. student
16.
17.
18.
19.
20.
21.
22.
23.
24.
25.

Name

Date

1. *cries*
2. *countries*
3. *families*
4. *stories*
5. *tried*
6. *hurried*
7. *carried*
8. *studied*
9. *prettier*
10. *earlier*
11. *easiest*
12. *luckily*
13. *happiness*
14. *business*
15. *beautiful*
16.
17.
18.
19.
20.
21.
22.
23.
24.
25.

List 47   Level E, List 11

Objective:

— Change **y** to **i** to add suffixes.

Rule: When a word ends in a consonant and y, change the y to i before adding a suffix unless the suffix begins with i. When a word ends in a vowel and y, do not change the y to i.

Review:

Review **play / plays / played, stay, destroy**. This rule does not apply when a word ends in a *vowel* and **y**.

Notes to the Teacher:

— Dictate these review words ending in **-y**.

try	family	stay	early
happy	day	story	lucky
fly	beauty	carry	hungry
cry	play	city	hurry
easy	ready	enemy	heavy
country	study	pretty	destroy

— Have students go through this list and cross out any words ending with a *vowel* and **y** (**-ay, -ey, -oy, -uy**). The rule here does *not* apply to these words. Suffixes are added in the normal way:

day / days

play / plays / played / playing

The other words end in a *consonant* and **y**. These are the words this rule governs.

— Teacher demonstration. **Cry + es**, erase the **y**, change it to **i** and add **-es**. Never add just **-s** to these words. How would you make **tries** from **try**? Do the same thing with **fly, carry, hurry, study**.

— Form plurals the same way: **family** to **families, story, city, enemy, country**.

— To add *any* suffix, do the same thing, *unless* it begins with an **i** such as **-ing** (**studiing** doesn't make sense). **Pretty + er = prettier, busy + ness = business, beauty + ful = beautiful, lucky + ly = luckily**. Review and reinforce this with many different words throughout the year. See Word Bank p. 147 for base words.

Level F Test

The emphasis in Level F is on silent letters, commonly misspelled words with multiple syllables, and the schwa sound in unaccented syllables.

1. ridge [54]	43. final [55]	84. twelve [49]	125. modern [51]
2. nineteen [49]	44. period [48]	85. guilty [56]	126. island [56]
3. tie [57]	45. doctor [57]	86. poor [53]	127. captain [49]
4. noise [48]	46. half [53]	87. rules [51]	128. safety [55]
5. impossible [54]	47. million [49]	88. nickel [58]	129. August [52]
6. attention [58]	48. special [55]	89. April [52]	130. nephew [50]
7. sister [50]	49. article [54]	90. uncle [50]	131. guess [56]
8. skiing [57]	50. son [50]	91. several [56]	132. hospital [51]
9. climb [53]	51. interest [57]	92. sentence [53]	133. pocket [58]
10. voice [48]	52. else [48]	93. office [48]	134. prairie [51]
11. character [54]	53. November [52]	94. absent [57]	135. entertain [49]
12. knowledge [54]	54. doubt [53]	95. library [52]	136. February [52]
13. father [50]	55. women [55]	96. northern [51]	137. listened [53]
14. children [55]	56. sincerely [55]	97. building [56]	138. December [52]
15. person [48]	57. dollar [58]	98. mountain [49]	139. question [58]
16. motor [57]	58. arctic [55]	99. barely [55]	140. forest [51]
17. answer [53]	59. edge [54]	100. July [52]	141. etc. [56]
18. thousand [49]	60. hundred [49]	101. niece [50]	142. forty [49]
19. social [55]	61. author [57]	102. language [56]	143. build [56]
20. simple [54]	62. point [48]	103. secretary [51]	144. medicine [53]
21. daughter [50]	63. stomach [54]	104. sense [58]	145. secret [51]
22. truly [57]	64. action [58]	105. stairs [51]	146. picture [58]
23. perfect [48]	65. brother [50]	106. certainly [49]	147. June [52]
24. October [52]	66. straight [57]	107. January [52]	148. cousin [50]
25. direction [58]	67. climbing [53]	108. listen [53]	149. fasten [53]
26. woman [55]	68. prison [48]	109. calendar [58]	150. probably [56]
27. since [55]	69. force [54]	110. speech [58]	151. practice [48]
28. regular [58]	70. table [54]	111. together [51]	152. bicycle [57]
29. argue [55]	71. grandma [50]	112. money [56]	153. all right [52]
30. bridge [54]	72. finally [55]	113. twenty-one [49]	154. pattern [51]
31. ninety [49]	73. perhaps [48]	114. built [56]	155. sign [56]
32. tying [57]	74. argument [57]	115. central [53]	156. certain [49]
33. noisy [48]	75. blood [53]	116. minute [51]	157. statement [55]
34. ache [54]	76. clothes [49]	117. figure [58]	158. September [52]
35. addition [58]	77. especially [55]	118. May [52]	159. relative [50]
36. mother [50]	78. possible [54]	119. aunt [50]	160. guard [56]
37. passed [57]	79. parents [50]	120. often [53]	161. enjoy [51]
38. climbed [53]	80. interesting [57]	121. toward [56]	162. ticket [58]
39. poison [48]	81. idea [48]	122. notice [48]	163. duty [51]
40. tragedy [54]	82. destroy [51]	123. gym [57]	164. eleven [49]
41. able [54]	83. key [56]	124. a lot [52]	165. March [52]
42. grandfather [50]			

Note: The superscript numbers indicate the *Spelling Plus* list for each word.

Name _____

Date _____

1. *noise*
2. *noisy*
3. *point*
4. *voice*
5. *poison*
6. *prison*
7. *person*
8. *period*
9. *perhaps*
10. *perfect*
11. *else*
12. *idea*
13. *office*
14. *notice*
15. *practice*
16. _____
17. _____
18. _____
19. _____
20. _____
21. _____
22. _____
23. _____
24. _____
25. _____

List 48   Level F, List 1

Words in Patterns:
— Words with **oi** as in **noise**, Word Bank p. 150.
— Words beginning with **per-**.

Notes to the Teacher:
— **Noise** and **noisy** can be linked.
— **Poison**, **prison**, and **person** end with **son** and can be linked. Mnemonics can be created such as, "My **son** knows a **person** who took **poison** in **prison**."
— **Person**, **period**, **perhaps** and **perfect** should be linked. Pronounce **period** to have the same first syllable sound as **perfect**. Point out to students that the word **purpose** is *not* in this pattern.
— **Office**, **notice**, and **practice** can be linked to **ice** with overpronunciation. To spell, say, **off - ice**, **not - ice**, **pract - ice**.
— Some possibilities for personal words: **avoid, toilet, viewpoint, moist, personal, personality, permit, permission, percent, perfume, service, justice, prejudice.**

Extension:
— Have students pluralize any words that can be pluralized: one **noise**, two **noises**.
— Add **-s** or **-es**, **-ed**, or **-ing** to any verbs: **points, pointed, pointing.**
— Add **-ly** to **perfect**.
— Add **-y** to **point**.
— Add **-ly** to **noisy** by changing **y** to **i** and adding the suffix.
— Add **-al** to **person**. Add **-ly** to **personal**. Add **-ity** to **personal**.

List 49   **Level F, List 2**

Words in Patterns:
— Words ending in **-ain**.
— Numbers and hyphens in numbers.

Homophones:
— **clothes / close** Teach if confusion exists.

Notes to the Teacher:
— Overpronounce words ending in **-ain** with a long **a** sound.
— The word **eight** has not yet been taught to mastery. It would be an excellent personal word for any students who don't know it.
— **Twelve** and **twenty** start like **two** but the **w** is pronounced. Put a hyphen in **twenty-one**, **twenty-two**, etc.
— There is no known reason why **forty** has no **u**. See the side bar on page 6 for more history.
— **Nineteen** and **ninety** keep the **e** when adding suffixes beginning with a consonant. This follows the rule. **Ninth** does *not* keep the silent **e**.
— **Clothes** can be thought of as **cloth + es**. **Clothes** are made of pieces of **cloth**.
— Possible personal words include: **fifteen, fifty, thirteen, thirty, ninety, curtain, bargain, fountain, villain, Britain**.

Extension:
— Challenge students to write words for the cardinal numbers from one to one hundred. Add **-teen** or **-ty** as needed. **Thirteen** and **thirty** have **thir** as in **third**. **Fifteen** and **fifty** have **fif** as in **fifth**. The rest are consistent.
— A more difficult challenge would be to write the ordinal numbers from **first** to **hundredth**. In many cases, **-th** is added to the cardinal number. **First, second, third, fourth, fifth, sixth . . . ninety-ninth, hundredth**. Sometimes, **y** must be changed to **i** as in **twentieth**.

Name

Date

1. mountain
2. captain
3. certain
4. certainly
5. entertain
6. eleven
7. twelve
8. twenty-one
9. forty
10. nineteen
11. ninety
12. hundred
13. thousand
14. million
15. clothes
16.
17.
18.
19.
20.
21.
22.
23.
24.
25.

Name

Date

1. *sister*
2. *mother*
3. *brother*
4. *father*
5. *grandfather*
6. *grandma*
7. *daughter*
8. *son*
9. *parents*
10. *uncle*
11. *aunt*
12. *cousin*
13. *niece*
14. *nephew*
15. *relative*
16.
17.
18.
19.
20.
21.
22.
23.
24.
25.

List 50   Level F, List 3

Words in Patterns:
— Words for family relations.

Homophones:
— **son** / **sun**
— **aunt** / **ant** (pronounced identically by some speakers)

Notes to the Teacher:
— Many of these words end in **-er**.
— **Daughter** is in the same pattern as **caught** and **taught**. Long ago, it rhymed with **laughter**.
— Overpronounce **cousin** with the **ou** sound in **out**.
— "My **niece** is **nice**." Generally, **i** comes before **e** except after **c**.
— **Nephew** has **ph** for the **f** sound. All words with **ph** are from Greek.
— **Relatives** are **related** to you. In **relate** the **a** sound is clearly heard.
— Personal words could include **couple**, **husband**, **wife**, **ex-husband**, **stepsister**, **brother-in-law**, **great-grandfather**, etc.

Extension:
— Have students add **step-**, **great-** or **ex-** to the beginnings of some of the words. Add **-in-law** to the ends of some words.
— Have students at home find the names of as many relatives as they can and write the relationship. Make a chart. Determine relationships from various points of view. This is an excellent time to teach apostrophes to show possession and begin using them in dictation: "Jim is John's uncle." "John is Jim's nephew."

List 51   Level F, List 4

Words in Patterns:
— Words with **-air** as in **stairs**, Word Bank p. 148.
— Words with **u** as in **duty**, Word Bank p. 150.
— Words ending in **-oy** as in **joy**, Word Bank p. 150.
— Words ending in **-ern** as in **northern**.
Guideline: Most common words end with -ary rather than -ery, with the exception of cemetery and stationery.

Homophones:
— **stairs** / **stares** Teach this set at this time.

Review:
— **air**, **fair**, **hair** from List 32.

Notes to the Teacher:
— **Prairie**. "There is **air** on the **prairie**."
— Link **duty** and **rules**. A teacher on recess **duty** enforces the **rules**.
— **Rules** is plural. What's the singular word?
— **Minute** with the accent on the first syllable is a noun, meaning 60 seconds. **Minute** with the accent on the second syllable is an adjective, meaning very small. A **minute** is a very small piece of time. Overpronounce this word as an adjective just to remember the spelling.
— A **secretary** can keep a **secret** (her boss' secrets). **-ary** means *connected with*.
— **Hospital** comes from **hospice** which is a guest room. Pronounce it carefully and correctly. It's *not* connected with **house**.
— **Forest**. Say **for - est**.
— "They went **together to - get - her**."
— Possible personal words include: **affair, repair, despair, western, southern, eastern, employ, tune, tube, rude, truth, super, stupid, brutal, rumor, substitute, attitude, reduce, introduce, suicide.**

Name

Date

1. stairs
2. prairie
3. duty
4. rules
5. minute
6. secret
7. secretary
8. hospital
9. enjoy
10. destroy
11. together
12. forest
13. northern
14. modern
15. pattern
16.
17.
18.
19.
20.
21.
22.
23.
24.
25.

Name

Date

1. January
2. February
3. March
4. April
5. May
6. June
7. July
8. August
9. September
10. October
11. November
12. December
13. library
14. a lot
15. all right
16.
17.
18.
19.
20.
21.
22.
23.
24.
25.

List 52
Level F, List 5

Words in Patterns:
— Names of the months, capitalized.

Notes to the Teacher:
— Make sure students can recite the months of the year in order. Upper grade teachers may incorrectly assume that students learned this earlier in their education.
— **February** and **library** can be linked with **br** (it's cold). Few people pronounce these words correctly. Exact pronunciation while spelling helps.
— **A lot**: "Do you want **a lot** or **a little**?"
— **All right**: "If it's not **all right**, it's **all wrong**."

Extension:
— Use this opportunity to have students memorize how many days are in each month. These mnemonics may help:
Thirty days hath September,
April, June and November.
All the rest have thirty-one
Except February, which has 28.
Or, have students make two fists and put them side by side. Knuckles protrude (31 days) and spaces between knuckles are lower (February and months with 30 days). The left knuckle is January (31), the space between the 1st and 2nd knuckles is February (28), the 2nd knuckle is March (31), etc. The two knuckles of the index fingers are side-by-side; July and August both have 31 days.
— The history of how months got their names is fascinating. A few facts: March was once the first month. Hence, **Sept**ember was seventh, **Oct**ober was eighth, **Nov**ember was ninth and **Dec**ember was tenth. Julius Caesar named **July** after himself. It used to be pronounced like **Julie**. Augustus Caesar named **August** after himself, and added a day to it by taking one from February.

List 53

Level F, List 6

Words in Patterns:
— Words with silent letters.
— Words with **oo** as in **blood**.
— Words with **oor** as in **poor**, Word Bank p. 148.

Notes to the Teacher:
— Have students clearly pronounce the silent letters as an aid to spelling.
— The **b** was added to **doubt** (and **debt**) in the 1600s. See the story on p. 6. In Middle English, it was spelled **dout** but its Latin root was **dubitare**. Latin was a revered language and this spelling revision stuck.
— **Climb** is from Middle English **climben**. Have students pronounce the **b** for spelling. **Limb, lamb, comb, bomb, tomb, numb, crumb, dumb** and **thumb** also end with silent **b**.
— **Medicine.** Link mentally to **medical**, which has the sound of hard **c**.
— Possible personal words include: **whistle, wrestle, glisten, debt, limb, lamb, comb, bomb, tomb, numb, crumb, dumb, thumb, flood, door, floor** and **medical**.

Extension:
— Add **-s** or **-es** to pluralize when possible. Note the irregular plural **half / halves**.
— Add **-s** or **-es**, **-ed**, and **-ing** to verbs.
— Add **-er** and **-est** to **poor**.
— Add **-y** to **blood**.
— Add **-ly** to **poor**.
— Add **-er**, meaning *a person or thing which*, to **fasten, listen, doubt,** and **climb**.

Name _____

Date _____

1. sentence
2. often
3. fasten
4. listen
5. listened
6. doubt
7. climb
8. climbed
9. climbing
10. answer
11. half
12. blood
13. poor
14. central
15. medicine
16.
17.
18.
19.
20.
21.
22.
23.
24.
25.

SPELLING LIST 54

Name
_____

Date
_____

1. *ridge*
2. *bridge*
3. *edge*
4. *knowledge*
5. *able*
6. *table*
7. *simple*
8. *article*
9. *possible*
10. *impossible*
11. *ache*
12. *stomach*
13. *character*
14. *tragedy*
15. *force*
16.
17.
18.
19.
20.
21.
22.
23.
24.
25.

List 54 Level F, List 7

Words in Patterns:
— Words ending with **-dge** as in **ridge**, Word Bank pp. 139–142.
— Words ending with **-le**.
— Words with **-ch** spelling the **k** sound.
Guideline: One of the most difficult problems in English spelling is **-able** *vs.* **-ible**. *Memorization is necessary. The following may be somewhat helpful:*
-able *is more common than* **-ible**.
-ible *is generally not added to a whole word (**break / breakable**)*
-ible *is used to keep a* **c** *or* **g** *soft (**eligible, invincible**). Since* **notice** *is a whole word,* **-able** *is added.* **Noticeable** *retains its* **e** *to keep the* **c** *soft.*
-ible *is used if a related word ends in* **-ion** *(**collection / collectible**)*

Notes to the Teacher:
— Have students try to pronounce the **d** in words with **-dge**. The tongue goes to the top of the mouth to pronounce these words. The **d** keeps the **g** soft and the **i** short. Otherwise, **ridge** would be **rige** with a long **i** or **rig** with a hard **g**.
— **Know** and **knowledge** should be linked.
— Point out that most words end in **-le** rather than **-el** but not all. **Nickel** ends with **-el**.
— **Ache**. See p. 6 for its story. Pronounce it **aitch** as in Shakespeare's time as an aid to spelling. Pronounce any and all **ch**'s with the sound in **ch**air as a memory aid.
— **Tragedy**, say **tra - ge - dy**.
— Possible personal words include: **badge**, **settle**, **battle**, **handle**, **tickle**, **trickle**, and **acknowledge**.

Extension:
— Pluralize by adding **-s** to nouns.
— Add **-er** and **-est** to **simple** by dropping the silent **e** and adding the suffix.

List 55

Level F, List 8

Objectives:
— Spell irregular plurals.
— Add suffixes **-ly** and **-ty**.

Homophones:
— **sense / since** Recommended to teach.

Notes to the Teacher:
— **Man / men.** The original meaning of **man** in English was "human being." The word did not mean a *male* human being until much later. German and Dutch words from the same root mean "people."
— **Woman / women.** The *pronunciation* is what is most irregular about **women**. It comes from the Old English word **wifman**. The sound of the first syllable changed for the singular form of the noun in the 1800s. The spelling changed for both singular and plural forms.
— **Child / children.** In Middle English, **-en** was an acceptable way to pluralize almost any word. See p. 5 for acceptable early ways to pluralize **cliff** (including **cliven**, **cliuenen**, and **clyuen**). Only **children**, **brethren**, and **oxen** preserve this.
— **Final + ly = finally.** This applies to all similar words.
— **Social,** say **so - ci - al.**
  Special, say **spe - ci - al.**
— **Especially,** say **e - special - ly.**
— Link **sin, since, sincerely.** "He doesn't **sin since** he **sincerely** changed."
— **Sincerely, barely, safety** and **statement** keep the silent **e** before a suffix beginning with a consonant. This follows the rule. Notable exceptions to this rule are **truly** and **argument.**
— Possible personal words include: **foot, feet, tooth, teeth, goose, geese, mouse, mice, official, financial, crucial, artificial, difficulty, certainty, cruelty, novelty.**

Name

Date

1. *woman*
2. *women*
3. *children*
4. *final*
5. *finally*
6. *social*
7. *special*
8. *especially*
9. *since*
10. *sincerely*
11. *barely*
12. *safety*
13. *statement*
14. *argue*
15. *arctic*
16.
17.
18.
19.
20.
21.
22.
23.
24.
25.

SPELLING LIST 56

Name _____

Date _____

1. several
2. toward
3. probably
4. language
5. guess
6. guard
7. guilty
8. built
9. build
10. building
11. island
12. sign
13. key
14. money
15. etc.
16. _____
17. _____
18. _____
19. _____
20. _____
21. _____
22. _____
23. _____
24. _____
25. _____

List 56   Level F, List 9

Words in Patterns:
— Words with silent letters.
— Words using **gu** to spell the sound of hard **g** and **bu** to spell the sound of **b**.
— Words ending in **-ey** as in **key**.

Notes to the Teacher:
— Overpronunciation is a key to remembering many of the words on this list. As an aid to spelling, pronounce the silent letters and enunciate all syllables.
  se - ver - al
  to - ward
  pro - ba - bly
  lan - gu - age
  gu - ess
  gu - ilty
  bu - ilt
  bu - ild
  bu - ilding
  is - land
  sig - n
— **Key**. Most words ending in the long **e** sound are spelled with **-e** as in **be**, or **-ee** as in **free**. See p. 144 for examples.
— **etc.** is an abbreviation for the Latin **et cetera**. Link with E.T. (extra terrestrial). In Latin **et** means *and* and **cetera** means *other things*. It is incorrect to write "and etc." because it is redundant. It means "and and other things."
— Possible personal words include: **guest, guide, guilt, guitar, valley, honey, monkey, donkey, turkey**, and **attorney**.

List 57   Level F, List 10

Words in Patterns:
— Words ending with **-or** as in **motor**.
— Words with **y** spelling short **i**.

Homophones:
— **passed** / **past** Important to teach.
— **straight** / **strait**
— **gym** / **Jim**

Notes to the Teacher:
— **Tie** / **tying** changes **ie** to **y**. Otherwise, it would be **tieing** with three consecutive vowels or **tiing**. **Tying** preserves the long **i** sound. **Die** / **dying** and **lie** / **lying** are also in this pattern.
— Link **author**, **motor** and **doctor** (**-or**).
— Neither **truly** nor **argument** keeps silent **e** according to the rule. These words must be memorized. Use frequently in dictation.
— **Arctic**, say **arc - tic**.
  Interesting, say **in - ter - est - ing**.
  Skiing, add **-ing** to **ski** for **ski - ing**. Each **i** has a separate sound.
  Passed, add **-ed** to **pass** for **pass - ed**.
  Absent, say **ab - sent**.
— **Straight** is irregular – rhymes with **eight**. It could be linked with **stray**: "The **stray** dog walked **stra**ight toward me."
— The homophones **passed** and **past** are very confusing. **Passed** is past tense of **pass**, and means *did pass*. In a sentence, if *did pass* can be substituted, use **passed**. Otherwise, use **past**. For example:
  She **passed** the test. She *did pass* the test.
  He **passed** the store. He *did pass* the store.
  He walked **past** the store. *Not:* He walked *did pass* the store.
  Kings ruled in the **past**. *Not:* Kings ruled in the *did pass*.
— Possible personal words include: **dying, lying, color, favor, flavor, honor, horror, terror, harbor, humor, mayor, visitor, director, sponsor, inventor,** and **tractor**.

Name _____

Date _____

1. tie
2. tying
3. author
4. motor
5. doctor
6. argument
7. truly
8. interest
9. interesting
10. skiing
11. passed
12. straight
13. absent
14. gym
15. bicycle
16.
17.
18.
19.
20.
21.
22.
23.
24.
25.

Name

Date

1. sense
2. pocket
3. ticket
4. nickel
5. figure
6. picture
7. speech
8. regular
9. dollar
10. calendar
11. question
12. direction
13. action
14. addition
15. attention
16.
17.
18.
19.
20.
21.
22.
23.
24.
25.

List 58   Level F, List 11

Words in Patterns:
— Words ending with **-et** and **-el**.
— Words ending with **-ure**.
— Words ending in **-ar**.
— Words ending in **-tion**.
*Guideline: **-el** is less common at the end of a word than **-le**.*

Homophones:
— **sense / since** Taught on List 55.
— **picture / pitcher** Teach if confused in writing.

Notes to the Teacher:
— Clearly pronounce the short **e** in **sense**, as it's pronounced in **send**. Contrast with the short **i** in **since**, with **i** as in **tin**.
— Link **nickel** with **pocket** and **ticket**.
— The **speech / speak** duo causes a lot of confusion. Why not **speach** (as in **teach**) and **speek** (as in **cheek**), or, even better, **speech / speek**? These words must simply be memorized. See the side bar on page 6 for some history on words with these sounds (the story of **ache**).
— Pronounce **re - gu - lar**, **doll - ar**, and **cal - en - dar** with the **-ar** heard in **car**.
— The letters **-tion** are common at the end of words. The same sound is sometimes spelled **-cion** as in **suspicion**.
— Possible personal words include: **market, target, bullet, blanket, jacket, rocket, planet, basket, carpet, cabinet, model, level, travel, novel, channel, tunnel, funnel, barrel, quarrel, label, angel, cancel, jewel, shovel, chapel, towel, pressure, nature, torture, feature, creature, injure, failure, capture, mixture, adventure, literature, temperature, furniture,** and **miniature**.

Level G Test

Pretest, Review, or Post-Test

The emphasis in Level G is on words frequently misspelled by high school students and adults. These are "spelling demons" for many people.

1. eight [62]
2. approach [65]
3. accept [59]
4. escape [63]
5. different [61]
6. occurrence [66]
7. recommend [65]
8. carefully [60]
9. scissors [69]
10. neighbor [62]
11. describe [64]
12. excuse [59]
13. criticize [67]
14. foreign [62]
15. possess [68]
16. independence [61]
17. area [66]
18. extremely [60]
19. scene [69]
20. incident [63]
21. disappoint [65]
22. distance [67]
23. excitement [59]
24. guarantee [63]
25. decide [68]
26. intelligent [61]
27. repetition [64]
28. realize [67]
29. profession [68]
30. weight [62]
31. opportunity [65]
32. except [59]
33. innocent [63]
34. difference [61]
35. equipped [66]
36. appear [65]
37. complete [60]
38. science [69]
39. leisure [62]
40. description [64]
41. excite [59]
42. criticism [67]

43. rhythm [62]
44. progress [68]
45. reference [61]
46. journal [66]
47. definite [60]
48. fascinate [69]
49. accident [63]
50. exaggerate [65]
51. acquaint [67]
52. example [59]
53. procedure [63]
54. discussion [68]
55. independent [61]
56. pronunciation [64]
57. recognize [67]
58. professor [68]
59. height [62]
60. necessary [65]
61. excellent [59]
62. difficult [63]
63. patient [61]
64. referred [66]
65. disappear [65]
66. completely [60]
67. conscience [69]
68. either [62]
69. repeat [64]
70. exciting [59]
71. perform [67]
72. grammar [62]
73. discuss [68]
74. existence [61]
75. machine [66]
76. definitely [60]
77. discipline [69]
78. accidentally [63]
79. accommodate [65]
80. acquaintance [67]
81. exercise [59]
82. generally [60]
83. affect [64]

84. occur [66]
85. lightning [61]
86. summary [67]
87. committee [65]
88. actual [60]
89. conscious [69]
90. relief [66]
91. receipt [62]
92. prepare [64]
93. occasion [68]
94. experience [59]
95. separate [63]
96. serious [69]
97. music [61]
98. appearance [67]
99. neither [62]
100. parallel [65]
101. mischievous [69]
102. usually [60]
103. concentrate [64]
104. principle [68]
105. develop [59]
106. particular [63]
107. college [66]
108. familiar [67]
109. convenient [61]
110. decided [68]
111. immediate [60]
112. effect [64]
113. occurring [66]
114. opinion [61]
115. apology [67]
116. embarrass [65]
117. actually [60]
118. nervous [69]
119. control [66]
120. seize [62]
121. continue [64]
122. success [68]
123. explain [59]
124. restaurant [63]

125. humorous [69]
126. misspell [61]
127. brilliant [67]
128. receive [62]
129. sandwich [65]
130. appreciate [69]
131. practical [60]
132. education [64]
133. principal [68]
134. development [59]
135. poem [63]
136. privilege [66]
137. identify [64]
138. responsible [63]
139. decision [68]
140. immediately [60]
141. suggest [64]
142. occurred [66]
143. benefit [61]
144. apologize [67]
145. opposite [65]
146. usual [60]
147. jealous [69]
148. commit [66]
149. weird [62]
150. imagine [64]
151. succeed [68]
152. expect [59]
153. similar [63]
154. continuous [69]
155. magazine [61]
156. peculiar [67]
157. deceive [62]
158. system [65]
159. delicious [69]
160. practically [60]
161. national [64]
162. physical [68]
163. government [59]
164. disease [63]
165. achieve [66]

Note: The superscript numbers indicate the *Spelling Plus* list for each word.

SPELLING LIST 59

Name

Date

1. accept
2. except
3. excellent
4. excuse
5. excite
6. exciting
7. excitement
8. example
9. exercise
10. experience
11. explain
12. expect
13. develop
14. development
15. government
16.
17.
18.
19.
20.
21.
22.
23.
24.
25.

List 59   Level G, List 1

Words in Patterns:
— Words beginning with **ex-**.
— Words ending with **-ment**.

Homophones:
— **accept** / **except** Recommended to teach.

Review:
— **statement** from List 55.

Notes to the Teacher:
— In **accept**, the prefix **ac-** means *to* or *towards*. In **except**, the prefix **ex-** means *out*. The root **cept** means *take*. Associate **accept** with **yes** (take towards), and **except** with **no** (take out).
— Overpronounce:
  ex - cel - lent
  ex - cuse
  ex - cite
  ex - am - ple
  ex - er - cise
  ex - per (as in period) **- i - ence**
  ex - plain
  ex - pect
— The suffix **-ment** means *state of being*. It is added directly to a base word, which normally keeps its silent **e**. **Argument** is an exception.
— Possible personal words include:
  experiment (link to **experience**), **department, movement, agreement, payment, environment, enjoyment, shipment, improvement, measurement, exist(ence), express(ion), extend, exact(ly), expense, examine, exchange, expand, expert, extra, expensive, explore, exhaust(ed), explode,** and **excellence**.

SPELLING LIST 60

Name

Date

List 60   Level G, List 2

Words in Patterns:
— Spell words ending with **-al**.
— Add **-ly** to base words.
Guideline: *-al is less common at the end of a word than **-le**.*

Review:
— **careful** and **awful** from List 38.
— **lucky** / **luckily** from Lists 45 and 47.
— **final** / **finally** from List 55.
— **sincerely** from List 55.
— **barely** from List 55.
— **special** / **especially** from List 55.

Notes to the Teacher:
— Many of the base words on this list are frequently misspelled. Try overpronouncing. The silent **e** was pronounced long ago and can be pronounced in these words as an aid to spelling.

    com - ple - te
    ex - tre - me
    def - in - i - te
    act - u - al
    us - u - al
    prac - ti - cal
    gen - er - al
    im - me - di - ate

— Add **-ly** without changing the base words. **Truly** is an exception.
— Possible personal words include: **total, general, legal, magical, medical, neutral, normal, original, arrival, signal, local, honestly, correctly, instantly, totally, recently, exactly, frequently, naturally, eventually, gradually, constantly, virtually, lately, normally, equally, promptly, currently, originally, roughly, commonly, instantly, correctly, silently, painfully, entirely, absolutely,** and **relatively.**

1. *carefully*
2. *complete*
3. *completely*
4. *extremely*
5. *definite*
6. *definitely*
7. *actual*
8. *actually*
9. *usual*
10. *usually*
11. *practical*
12. *practically*
13. *generally*
14. *immediate*
15. *immediately*
16.
17.
18.
19.
20.
21.
22.
23.
24.
25.

SPELLING LIST 61

Name _____

Date _____

1. music
2. misspell
3. magazine
4. lightning
5. opinion
6. benefit
7. different
8. difference
9. patient
10. intelligent
11. independent
12. independence
13. reference
14. existence
15. convenient
16.
17.
18.
19.
20.
21.
22.
23.
24.
25.

List 61   Level G, List 3

Words in Patterns:
— Words ending with **-ent** and **-ence**.
*Guideline: Knowing whether to use **-ence** or **-ance** is a difficult spelling problem. If the base word ends with **-ent**, **-ence** is correct. If the base word ends with **-ant**, **-ance** is correct. Words ending in **-ance** are taught on List 67.*

Homophones:
— **patience** / **patients**   Good time to teach.

Notes to the Teacher:
— **Music** once had a **k** at the end. It was dropped as useless by Noah Webster.
— **Mis-** is a prefix meaning *wrong* or *bad*.
  Mis + spell = misspell with **ss**. Imagine a Little Miss Pell.
— Overpronounce the following words, giving the schwa sounds their full value.

mag - a - zine	**in - tell - i - gent**
light - ning	**in - de - pen - dent**
o - pin - i - on	**re - fer - ence**
ben - e - fit	**ex - ist - ence**
dif - fer - ent	**con - ven - i - ent**
pat - i - ent	

— Some mnemonics:
  Tell me I'm in**tell**igent.
  There is a **dent** in indepen**dent**.
— Possible personal words are **public**, **coincidence**, **impatient**, **quotient** or any of the following:

present / **presence**	absent / **absence**
silent / **silence**	**patient** / **patience**
evident / **evidence**	violent / **violence**
resident / **residence**	
excellent / **excellence**	
intelligent / **intelligence**	
confident / **confidence**	
convenient / **convenience**	
permanent / **permanence**	
persistent / **persistence**	
magnificent / **magnificence**	
correspondent / **correspondence**	

Note that words not in bold type here are on the core list.

List 62   Level G, List 4

Words in Patterns:
— Words with **ei** as in **eight**.
— Words with **rh** as in **rhythm**.
Rule: *Write **i** before **e** except after **c**,*
*or when sounded like **a***
*as in n**ei**ghbor and w**ei**gh*
*(This doesn't apply when the sound of **ci***
*is **sh** as in **ancient**. See List 69.)*

Homophones:
— **ate** / **eight** Teach or review.

Notes to the Teacher:
— Have students find words in the list that
follow the rule above and mark any
words that don't. Those that don't are
**height, leisure, either, neither, seize,
weird, foreign** (from **reign**, which does
follow the rule).
— Almost all common words that do not
follow the **i** before **e** rule are on this
spelling list.
— Link **eight** and **weight**, **eight** and **height**.
His **weight** was **eight** hundred pounds.
His **height** was **eight** feet.
— Link **receive** and **deceive**.
— Link **receive** and **receipt**. **Receipt** was
once spelled **receite**. The **p** was added
in the 1600s to reflect the Latin **recepta**.
Receptacle and **reception** come from the
same root.
— **We** are w**e**ird.
— **Rhythm** is originally from Greek, as is
rhyme.
— **Gramma** knows her **grammar**.
— Possible personal words include: **rhyme,
weigh, reign, rein, reindeer, sleigh, veil,
vein, neigh, freight, ceiling, conceited,
deceive, perceive, conceive, caffeine,
protein, forfeit, counterfeit,** and **surfeit**.

Name _____

Date _____

1. eight
2. weight
3. height
4. neighbor
5. leisure
6. either
7. neither
8. deceive
9. receive
10. receipt
11. seize
12. weird
13. foreign
14. rhythm
15. grammar
16. _____
17. _____
18. _____
19. _____
20. _____
21. _____
22. _____
23. _____
24. _____
25. _____

SPELLING LIST 63

Name

Date

1. incident
2. accident
3. accidentally
4. escape
5. innocent
6. difficult
7. guarantee
8. procedure
9. responsible
10. separate
11. restaurant
12. similar
13. particular
14. poem
15. disease
16.
17.
18.
19.
20.
21.
22.
23.
24.
25.

List 63　　Level G, List 5

Objective:
— Spell "demons."
Guideline: One of the most difficult problems in English spelling is -able vs. -ible. Memorization is necessary. The following may be somewhat helpful:
-able is more common than -ible.
-ible is generally not added to a whole word (break / breakable)
-ible is used to keep a c or g soft (eligible, invincible). Since notice is a whole word, -able is added. Noticeable retains its e to keep the c soft.
-ible is used if a related word ends in -ion (collection / collectible)

Notes to the Teacher:
— Overpronounce difficult words:
  in - ci - dent
  ac - ci - dent
  ac - ci - dent - al - ly (from **accidental**)
  es - cape
  in - no - cent (three little words)
  diff - i - cult
  gu - ar - an - tee
  pro - ced - ure
  re - spon - si - ble
  rest - au - rant
  sim - i - lar
  part - i - cu - lar
  po - em
  dis - ease (**dis-** is a prefix meaning *not*)
— **Proceed** has two e's, while **procedure** has just one. Memorize.
— Mnemonic: sep - **a** - rat**e a rat**
— Link **guarantee** and **guess**.
— Possible personal words include: **tongue, vague, fatigue, incredible, flexible, visible, invisible, sensible** and **horrible**.

Extension:
— Add **-ly** to **innocent, separate, similar,** and **particular**.
— Add **-y** to **difficult**.

List 64   Level G, List 6

Objective:
— Add **-ion**, **-tion** or **-ation** to words, making nouns from verbs.

Homophones:
— **Affect** is a verb meaning *to influence* and **effect** is generally a noun meaning *a result*. **Effect** is much less frequently used as a verb meaning *to bring about*. There is no need to introduce the verb to students now as it may confuse them.

Notes to the Teacher:
— Most words on this list either end in **-tion** or are base words to which **-ion**, **-tion**, or **-ation** can be added:
   affect / affection
   suggest / suggestion
   prepare / preparation
   continue / continuation
   imagine / imagination
   concentrate / concentration
   educate / education
— Some words change the spelling in the base word. These are frequently misspelled. Careful pronunciation can help.
   describe (long **i**) / **description** (short **i**)
   repeat (long **e**) / **repetition** (short **e**)
   pronounce (ou) / **pronunciation** (schwa)
   identify / identification (changes **y** to **i** and adds **-cation**)
— Some words from previous lessons:
   explain / explanation
   except / exception
   deceive / deception
   receive / reception
— Possible personal words include:
   affection, **suggestion**, **preparation**, **continuation**, **imagination**, **concentration**, **educate**, **pronounce**, **identification**, **explanation**, **exception**, **deception**, **reception**, and **competition**.

Name _____

Date _____

1. affect
2. effect
3. suggest
4. prepare
5. continue
6. imagine
7. concentrate
8. education
9. national
10. describe
11. description
12. repeat
13. repetition
14. pronunciation
15. identify
16.
17.
18.
19.
20.
21.
22.
23.
24.
25.

SPELLING LIST 65

Name

Date

1. approach
2. opportunity
3. necessary
4. recommend
5. appear
6. disappear
7. disappoint
8. exaggerate
9. accommodate
10. committee
11. embarrass
12. opposite
13. parallel
14. sandwich
15. system
16.
17.
18.
19.
20.
21.
22.
23.
24.
25.

List 65   Level G, List 7

Words in Patterns:
— Difficult words with double letters.
— Words using **y** to spell short **i** sound.
Guideline: Most common words end with
  ***-ary** rather than **-ery**, with the exception*
  *of **cemetery** and **stationery**.*

Review:
— **Secretary** from List 51.

Notes to the Teacher:
— The double letters in these words make them demons. Provide lots of practice and review.
— Mnemonic: **Accommodate** can accommodate many sets of twin letters.
— Mnemonic: **Committee** has three sets of twin letters.
— Mnemonic: Not **all** lines are par**all**el.
— Possible personal words include: **appoint, appointment, vacuum, balloon, symbol, sympathy, symphony, symptom, typical, mystery, myth, crystal, oxygen, hymn, dictionary, primary, elementary, temporary, secondary, military, ordinary, missionary,** and **vocabulary.**

Extending the Lesson:
— This may be a good time to teach the homophones **stationary / stationery** and have some students study them as personal words. Notice the **er** in **stationery**. **Letter** also has **er**. You write a lett**er** on station**er**y.
— **Cemetery** is another possible personal word. Mnemonic: You go to the c**e**m**e**t**e**ry with **e**'s (ease).

List 66   Level G, List 8

Words in Patterns:
— Words ending with **-ege**. These are often confused with words ending with **-edge**.
— Words with **ie** as in **relief**, p. 144.
— Two-syllable words with the accent on the last syllable. Adding suffixes.

Notes to the Teacher:
— Students frequently spell **college** and **privilege** with a **d** as in **knowledge**. Link these two words and memorize them. It's a **privilege** to go to **college**. **Privilege** comes from the roots *leg* (as in **legal**) and *priv* (as in **private**). A **privilege** is a special law not made for everyone.
— **Achieve** and **relief** follow the **i** before **e** rule (p. 129). **Relieve** and **receive** may cause confusion. Note the **c** in **receive**.
— **Control**, **commit**, **occur**, **equip**, and **refer** have the accent on the last syllable, as does **begin**. Because of this, the final consonant is doubled before endings beginning with a vowel (**-ed**, **-ing**, **-ence**), but not with a consonant (**-s**, **-ment**).
control / controlled / controlling
commit / committed / committing
occur / occurred / occurring / occurrence
equip / equipped / equipping / equipment
refer / refers / referred / referring
— Possible personal words: **journey**, **relieve**, **reprieve** and any words below.

Extension:
— Mix the following words on the board and have students determine which are accented on the last syllable. Add endings: **patrol, admit, rebel, dispel, repel, compel, commit, concur, occur, refer, annul, expel, control, regret, prefer, equip, deter, forget, excel, profit, travel, counsel, cancel, worship, signal, marvel, kidnap, suffer.**

Name

Date

1. college
2. privilege
3. achieve
4. relief
5. control
6. commit
7. occur
8. occurring
9. occurred
10. occurrence
11. equipped
12. referred
13. area
14. journal
15. machine
16.
17.
18.
19.
20.
21.
22.
23.
24.
25.

SPELLING LIST 67

Name _____

Date _____

1. summary
2. apology
3. apologize
4. realize
5. recognize
6. criticize
7. criticism
8. perform
9. distance
10. acquaint
11. acquaintance
12. appearance
13. brilliant
14. peculiar
15. familiar
16. _____
17. _____
18. _____
19. _____
20. _____
21. _____
22. _____
23. _____
24. _____
25. _____

List 67   Level G, List 9

Words in Patterns:
— Words ending with **-ize**.
— Words ending with **-ant** and **-ance**.
Guideline: Few common words end with **-ise**. *With the exception of* **surprise, exercise, advertise,** *and* **revise,** *common words with this final sound end in* **-ize**. *Paralyze and analyze are the only common words ending in* **-yze**.

Notes to the Teacher:
— The suffix **-ize** means *to cause to resemble*. It is often spelled **-ise** in England. **Surprise** ends in **-ise**.
— Spellers often confuse **-ant** and **-ent**, as well as **-ance** and **-ence**. All words on this list end with **-ance**. Students must memorize which is which or use a dictionary. See List 61 for some guidelines.
— **Brilliant, peculiar** and **familiar** have a **y** sound spelled with **i**. Listen for it.
— Mnemonics: a pecu**liar liar**, a fami**liar liar**.
— **Family** and **familiar** can be linked.
— Additional pairs (possible personal words)
brilliant / **brilliance**
perform / **performance**
allow / **allowance**
attend / attendant / attendance
instant / instance
assistant / assistance
reluctant / reluctance
elegant / elegance
insure / insurance
ignore / ignorance

Note that words not in bold type here are on the core list.

— Other possible personal words include: **constant, servant, Protestant, elephant, sergeant, infant, vacant, finance, balance, circumstance, entrance, substance, organize, emphasize, specialize, characterize, criticize, generalize, summarize, minimize, utilize, civilize, analyze,** and **paralyze.**

List 68   Level G, List 10

Words in Patterns:
— Words ending with **-al**.
— Words ending with **-ss** and **-sion**.
Guideline: -cede is the most common spelling of this root, meaning "go." Only three words end with -ceed: succeed, proceed, and exceed. Only one word ends with -sede: supersede.

Homophones:
— **principle / principal** Note that **le** ends both **rule** and **principle**. Any rule, truth, or pattern of conduct is a **principle**. Use **principal** for all other meanings. The word **main** has an **a** as in **principal**. The **principal** of a loan is the main part. A school **principal** is the main leader.

Notes to the Teacher:
— **Physical** and all words with **ph** spelling the **f** sound are from Greek. Spellings were retained to show the derivation in English, but not in most other languages. In Spanish, the word is spelled **fisical**.
— **Decide** has the same root as **suicide** and **homicide**. The root **cide** means *to kill*.
— Usually, base words end with **-ss** not a single **-s**. Most words ending with a single **s** are either pluralized or inflected.
— **Professor**. An exam at New Jersey's Fairleigh Dickinson University showed that less than a quarter of their freshman class could spell this word correctly!
— Possible personal words include: **exceed, proceed, dismiss, session, possession, mission, division, invasion, explosion, collision, confusion, tension, television, version, permission, professional** and:
process / procession
express / expression
impress / impression
depress / depression
confess / confession
compress / compression.

Name

Date

1. *principle*
2. *principal*
3. *physical*
4. *decide*
5. *decided*
6. *decision*
7. *occasion*
8. *success*
9. *succeed*
10. *profession*
11. *professor*
12. *possess*
13. *progress*
14. *discuss*
15. *discussion*
16.
17.
18.
19.
20.
21.
22.
23.
24.
25.

SPELLING LIST 69

Name

Date

1. scene
2. fascinate
3. discipline
4. scissors
5. science
6. conscience
7. conscious
8. nervous
9. jealous
10. serious
11. humorous
12. continuous
13. mischievous
14. delicious
15. appreciate
16.
17.
18.
19.
20.
21.
22.
23.
24.
25.

List 69   Level G, List 11

Words in Patterns:
— Words using **sc** to spell the sound of **s**.
— Words ending with **-ous**.
— Words using **ci** to spell sound of **sh**.
Rule: *The **i** before **e** rule doesn't apply when **ci** is pronounced as **sh**.*

Homophones:
— **scene / seen** Students will not normally confuse these two.

Notes to the Teacher:
— The **sh** sound is one of the most difficult to spell: **appreciate, luscious, sugar, passion, fashion, patient.**
— **Con - science** can be linked with **science**.
— The suffix **-ous** means *full of* or *having*. Generally, the sound of **us** is spelled **-ous** at the end of a word.
— Clearly pronounce every letter in **mis - chi - e - vous**.
— Possible personal words with **sc**: **scientific, scientist, muscle, descend, descent, scenery, adolescent,** and **luscious**.
— Possible personal words with **ci**: **official, associate, ancient, musician, artificial, suspicion, species, glacier, proficient, deficient, efficient,** and **sufficient**.
— Possible personal words with **-ous**: **famous, dangerous, anxious, various, mysterious, marvelous, religious, continuous, courteous, obvious, miscellaneous, previous, curious, numerous, tremendous, enormous, precious, generous, suspicious, ridiculous, monstrous, glorious, cautious,** and **delicious**. Retain the final silent **e** to keep the soft **g** in **gorgeous** and **courageous**.

WORD BANK

This Word Bank has been prepared to help teachers extend the basic lessons in *Spelling Plus*. Words in the same patterns as those on basic lists can be personal words. Any regularly spelled words can be used in dictation after the pattern has been introduced.

The best use of words in the Word Bank may be to extend the application of rules to a large number of regularly spelled words. For example, pp. 138–142 have lists of one-syllable words with short vowels. These can be used as a resource for dictating words needing a doubled consonant such as *tagged, sadder,* and *clapped.* Lists of one-syllable words with long vowels are on pp. 143–146. Dictate words requiring the dropping of silent **e** such as *joking, taped,* and *glider.* A list of words ending in **y** is on p. 147. Have students practice changing **y** to **i** and adding endings.

Irregularly spelled words are listed under "Other" along with regularly spelled words that are unique.

ă

–ab	–ag	–am	–an	–at	–as	–ack
blab	bag	am	an	at	*(Generally spelled –ass as in pass.)*	back
cab	brag	clam	ban	bat	as	black
crab	crag	cram	bran	brat	gas	clack
dab	drag	dam	can	cat	has	crack
drab	flag	ham	clan	chat		hack
flab	gag	jam	Dan	fat		Jack
gab	lag	Pam	fan	flat	**–ash**	knack
grab	nag	ram	Fran	hat	bash	lack
jab	rag	Sam	Jan	mat	brash	Mack
lab	sag	sham	man	Nat	cash	pack
nab	shag	scram	Nan	pat	clash	quack
scab	snag	slam	pan	Pat	crash	rack
slab	stag	swam	plan	rat	dash	sack
stab	tag	Tam	ran	sat	flash	shack
tab	wag	yam	scan	scat	gash	slack
			span	slat	hash	smack
			Stan	that	lash	snack
			tan	vat	mash	stack
	–al	**–amp**	than		rash	tack
–ad	Al	camp	van	**–ath**	sash	track
ad	gal	champ		bath	slash	whack
bad	Hal	clamp	**–and**	math	smash	
Brad	pal	cramp	and	path	smash	
Chad	Val	damp	band		stash	
clad		gramp	bland	**–act**	trash	**–ass**
dad	**–ap**	lamp	brand	act	thrash	bass
fad	cap	ramp	brand	fact		brass
glad	chap	scamp	grand	tact		class
had	clap	stamp	hand		**–ask**	glass
lad	flap	tramp	land		ask	grass
mad	gap		sand	**–ance**	bask	lass
pad	lap		stand	dance	cask	mass
sad	map	**–atch**	strand	chance	flask	pass
scad	nap	batch		glance	mask	
Tad	rap	catch		prance	task	
	sap	hatch	**–ant**	stance		**–aff**
–aft	scrap	latch	ant	trance	**–ast**	chaff
craft	slap	match	chant		blast	staff
daft	snap	patch	grant	**–ax**	cast	
draft	strap	scratch	pant	ax	fast	**–asp**
raft	tap	snatch	plant	lax	last	clasp
shaft	trap		rant	Max	mast	gasp
Taft	wrap		scant	tax	past	hasp
	yap		slant		vast	rasp

Other:
add
after
badge
branch
cabin
calf
gasp
graph
half
lamb
laugh
laughter
plaid
plaque
rabbit
ranch
scalp
shall
shallow
wagon

–eb
Deb
web

–ed
bed
bled
Ed
fed
fled
Fred
Jed
led
Ned
red
shed
sled
sped
Ted
wed

–eg
beg
Greg
keg
leg
Meg
peg
Peg

–eld
held
weld

–elf
elf
self
shelf

–elp
help
kelp
yelp

–elt
belt
felt
knelt
melt
pelt
welt

–em
Clem
gem
hem
stem
them

–ep
pep
Shep
strep

–ept
crept
kept
swept
wept

–ence
fence
hence

–ense
dense
sense
tense

–ench
bench
clench
drench
French
quench
stench
trench

–en
Ben
den
Glen
hen
Ken
men
pen
ten
then
when
yen

–end
bend
blend
end
fend
lend
mend
rend
send
spend
tend
trend
vend
wend

–ent
bent
Brent
cent
dent
lent
rent
scent
sent
spent
tent
Trent
vent
went

–et
bet
get
jet
let
met
net
pet
set
vet
wet
yet

–etch
etch
fetch
sketch
stretch
wretch

–edge
dredge
edge
hedge
ledge
sledge
wedge

–esh
flesh
mesh
thresh

–est
best
chest
crest
nest
pest
quest
rest
test
vest
west
zest

–ex
flex
hex
Rex
vex

–eck
check
deck
fleck
neck
peck
wreck

–ess
Bess
bless
dress
Jess
less
mess
press
stress
Tess

–ell
bell
cell
fell
hello
quell
sell
shell
smell
spell
swell
tell
well
yell

ĕ

Other:
again
against
any
been
Beth
debt
desk
elk
else
ever
every
friend
guess
Jeff
left
many
never
next
said
seven
whether
yes

Spelled ea

ahead
bread
breakfast
breast
breath
dead
deaf
dealt
death
dread
feather
head

health
heaven
heavy
instead
leather
meadow
meant
measure
pleasant
pleasure
read
ready

spread
steady
stealth
sweat
sweater
thread
threaten
tread
treasure
wealthy
weapon
weather

140

ĭ

Other:
build
built
filth
fizz
guilty
his
if
is
limb
mitt
quiz
rich
rinse
this
which
whiz
wind

Spelled y
bicycle
crystal
gym
gyp
hymn
mystery
myth
oxygen
rhythm
symbol
sympathy
symphony
symptom
system
typical

–ib
bib
crib
fib
rib

–id
bid
did
grid
hid
kid
lid
rid
Sid
skid
slid

–ift
drift
gift
lift
rift
sift
shift
swift
thrift

–ig
big
dig
fig
gig
jig
pig
rig
sprig
swig
twig
wig

–ilt
hilt
kilt
lilt
quilt
silt
stilt
tilt
wilt

–im
brim
dim
grim
him
Jim
Kim
rim
skim
slim
swim
Tim
trim

–imp
blimp
chimp
limp
skimp
scrimp

–ip
chip
clip
dip
drip
flip
grip
hip
lip
nip
quip
rip
sip
ship
skip
slip
snip
strip
tip
trip
whip
yip
zip

–in
bin
chin
din
fin
gin
grin
in
kin
pin
sin
shin
skin
spin
tin
thin
twin
win

–inch
cinch
inch
pinch
winch

–ince
mince
prince
since
wince

–int
flint
glint
hint
lint
mint
print
stint
sprint
tint

–it
bit
fit
flit
grit
hit
it
kit
knit
lit
pit
quit
sit
skit
slit
spit
wit

–ith
Smith
with

–itch
ditch
hitch
itch
kitchen
pitch

stitch
switch
twitch
witch

–idge
bridge
ridge

–ix
fix
mix
six

–ish
dish
fish
swish
Trish
wish

–isk
brisk
disk
risk
whisk

–ist
fist
list
mist
twist
wrist

–ill
Bill
chill
dill
drill
fill
frill
grill
hill
Jill
kill
mill
pill
quill
sill
skill
spill
still
thrill
will

–ick
brick
chick
click
Dick
flick
hick
kick
lick
Mick
nick
Nick
pick
quick
Rick
sick
slick
stick
tick
thick
trick
wick

–iss
bliss
hiss
kiss
miss
Swiss

–iff
cliff
skiff
sniff
stiff
whiff

–ob	**–og**	**–om**	**–op**	**–ot**	**–osh**	**–ock**	**Ŏ**
blob	bog	mom	chop	blot	gosh	block	
Bob	clog	prom	cop	clot	posh	clock	
cob	cog	Tom	crop	cot	slosh	crock	
glob	dog		drop	dot		dock	
gob	flog	**–omp**	flop	got		flock	
job	fog	chomp	hop	hot	**–ost**	hock	*Other:*
knob	frog	romp	lop	jot	cost	knock	are
mob	hog	stomp	mop	lot	frost	lock	author
rob	jog		plop	not	lost	mock	body
slob	log	**–on**	pop	plot		rock	bomb
snob	slog	con	prop	plot		shock	broad
sob	smog	Don	top	pot	**–ox**	smock	copy
throb		Ron	shop	rot	box	sock	father
		on	slop	shot	fox	Spock	gone
–od	**–otch**		stop	slot	pox		John
clod	blotch			spot			off
cod	botch	**–ond**				**–oss**	
God	notch	blond				boss	
nod	scotch	bond			**–oll**	cross	
plod		fond			doll	floss	
pod		pond			golly	gloss	
prod	**–odge**				jolly	loss	
rod	dodge				Molly	moss	
shod	lodge				Polly	toss	
sod							
trod							

–oft	**–au**		**–all**	**–alm**
loft	applaud		all	almond
soft	applause		ball	alms
	audience		call	calm
–a	author		fall	palm
ma	auto		hall	psalm
pa	autumn	**–aw**	mall	qualm
spa	because	awful	small	
	cause	bawl	stall	**wa–**
	caution	brawl	swallow	wad
–augh	exhaust	caw	tall	waft
caught	fault	claw	wall	wand
daughter	flaunt	crawl		want
distraught	gaunt	dawn	**–alk**	wash
fraught	haul	draw	chalk	watch
naughty	haunt	drawer	stalk	water
onslaught	launch	drawl	talk	swat
slaughter	Paul	drawn	walk	swap
taught	pause	fawn		swan
	sauce	flaw		swamp
–ough	taunt	gnaw		
bought		jaw		
brought		law		
cough		lawyer		
fought		lawn		
ought		paw		
sought		pawn		
thought		raw		
trough		saw		
		scrawl		
		Shaw		
		shawl		
		sprawl		
		spawn		
		squaw		
		straw		
		yawn		

142

ŭ

Other:
a
among
blood
come
does
done
flood
from
front
month
much
none
of
once
one
other
second
some
son
such
the
ton
under
was
what

–ub
club
cub
grub
hub
rub
scrub
snub
stub
sub
tub

–ud
bud
crud
cud
dud
mud
scud
spud
stud
thud

–ug
bug
chug
dug
glug
hug
jug
lug
mug
plug
rug
shrug
slug
smug
snug
thug
tug

–up
cup
pup
up

–um
bum
chum
drum
glum
gum
hum
plum
rum
scum
slum
strum
sum
swum
yum

–ump
bump
clump
dump
grump
hump
jump
lump
mump
plump
pump
rump
slump
stump
thump
trump

–un
bun
fun
gun
nun
pun
run
shun
spun
stun
sun

–unt
blunt
brunt
grunt
punt
runt
stunt

–unch
brunch
bunch
crunch
hunch
lunch
munch
punch

–ut
but
cut
glut
gut
hut
jut
nut
rut
shut
strut

–utch
clutch
crutch
Dutch
hutch

–udge
drudge
fudge
grudge
judge
nudge
sludge
smudge
trudge

–ou
couple
cousin
double
enough
rough
touch
tough
trouble
young

–ush
blush
brush
crush
flush
gush
hush
lush
mush
plush
rush
shush
slush

–usk
dusk
husk
musk
tusk

–ust
bust
crust
dust
gust
just
must
rust
thrust
trust

–us
bus
Gus
plus
pus
us

–uck
buck
Chuck
cluck
duck
luck
muck
pluck
puck
shuck
struck
stuck
suck
truck
tuck
yuck

–uss
fuss
Russ

–uff
bluff
cuff
fluff
gruff
huff
puff
stuff

–ull
dull
gull
hull
lull

–umb
crumb
dumb
numb
thumb

ve

Other:
grieve
heave
leave
peeve
sleeve
Steve
weave

–ave
brave
cave
crave
Dave
gave
grave
have
pave
rave
save
shave
slave
wave

–ove
above
clove
cove
drove
dove
glove
grove
love
move
prove
rove
shove
stove
wove

–ive
chive
dive
drive
five
give
hive
live
strive
thrive
wives

–abe
babe
Gabe

–ade
blade
fade
glade
grade
jade
made
shade
trade
wade

–age
age
cage
page
rage
sage
stage
wage

–ape
cape
drape
gape
grape
nape
scrape
shape
tape

–ame
blame
came
dame
fame
flame
frame
game
James
lame
name
same
shame
tame

–ane
cane
crane
Jane
lane
mane
pane
plane
sane
Shane
vane
wane

–ange
change
range
strange

–ate
ate
crate
date
fate
grate
hate
Kate
late
mate
Nate
plate
rate
skate
slate
state

–ale
bale
Dale
male
pale
sale
shale
stale
tale
whale

–aste
baste
haste
taste
waste

–ake
bake
Blake
brake
cake
fake
flake
Jake
lake
make
quake
rake
sake
shake
snake
stake
take
wake

ā

Other:
ache
bathe
break
great
hey
safe
straight
steak
they
waist

–aid
afraid
braid
laid
maid
paid
raid

–ay
away
bay
bray
clay
day
fray
gay
gray
hay
jay
Kay
lay
may
pay
play

pray
ray
Ray
say
slay
spray
stay
stray
sway
today
tray
way

–aim
claim
maim

ei
deign
reign
rein
reindeer
veil
vein

eigh
eight
freight
neigh
neighbor
sleigh
weigh
weight

–ain
brain
chain
drain
gain
grain
main
pain
plain
rain
slain
Spain
sprain
stain
strain
train
vain

–ait
bait
gait
trait
wait

–aise
braise
praise
raise

–aint
faint
paint
quaint
saint

–ail
bail
fail
flail
frail
Gail
hail
jail
mail
nail
pail
quail
rail
sail
snail
tail
trail
wail

–ase
base
case
chase
vase

–ace
brace
face
grace
lace
pace
place
race
space
trace

–aze
blaze
faze
gaze
glaze
graze
maze

144

ē

Other:
breathe
fleece
leaf
leash
peace
people
scene
seem
teeth
these

–e
be
he
me
she
we

–ee
bee
fee
flee
free
gee
glee
knee
lee
see
spree
three
tree
whee

–ea
flea
plea
sea
tea

–ead
bead
lead
plead
read

–eed
bleed
breed
creed
deed
feed
greed
heed
need
reed
seed
speed
steed
tweed
weed

–eek
cheek
creek
Greek
meek
peek
reek
seek
sleek
week

–eak
beak
bleak
creak
freak
leak
peak
sneak
speak
squeak
streak
teak
weak

–eef
beef
reef

–eel
feel
heel
keel
kneel
peel
reel
wheel

–eal
conceal
deal
ideal
heal
meal
peal
real
reveal
seal
steal
veal

–eam
beam
cream
dream
gleam
ream
scream
seam
steam
stream
team

–een
green
keen
queen
seen
screen
sheen
teen

–eep
beep
creep
deep
jeep
keep
peep
seep
sheep
sleep
steep
sweep
weep

–ean
bean
clean
Dean
glean
Jean
lean
mean
wean

–eap
cheap
heap
leap
reap

–eet
beet
feet
fleet
greet
meet
sheet
sleet
street
sweet
tweet

–eech
beech
leech
screech
speech

–eat
beat
bleat
cheat
cleat
defeat
eat
heat
meat
neat
peat
repeat
retreat
seat
treat
wheat

–each
beach
bleach
breach
each
leach
peach
preach
reach
teach

–eese
cheese
geese

–eeze
breeze
freeze
sneeze
squeeze

–eeve
peeve
sleeve

–eas
beast
cease
crease
decrease
ease
east
Easter
easy
feast
grease
increase
lease
least
please
reason
release
season
tease
yeast

–eave
heave
leave
weave
heave

–ei
caffeine
ceiling
conceit
conceive
deceive
either
Keith
leisure
Neil
neither
perceive
protein
receipt
receive
seize
Sheila

–ey
honey
key
money
monkey
valley

–ie
achieve
belief
believe
brief
chief
field
grief
grieve
niece
piece
priest
relief
relieve
shriek
thief
yield

ī

–ibe
bribe
scribe
tribe

–ide
bride
glide
hide
pride
ride
slide
side
stride
tide
wide

–ipe
gripe
pipe
ripe
stripe
swipe
tripe
wipe

–ife
knife
life
strife
wife

–ime
chime
crime
dime
grime
lime
prime
slime
time

–ine
brine
dine
fine
line
mine
nine
pine
shine
shrine
spine
swine
twine
vine
wine
whine

–ind
bind
blind
find
grind
hind
kind
mind
wind

–ile
awhile
file
mile
Nile
pile
smile
tile
vile
while

–ild
child
mild
wild

–ire
fire
hire
mire
spire
tire
wire

–ite
bite
kite
quite
spite
trite
white
write

–ise
rise
surprise
wise

–ize
prize
size

–ike
bike
dike
hike
like
Mike
pike
spike
strike

–ice
dice
ice
lice
mice
nice
price
rice
slice
spice
twice
vice

Other:
climb
eye
height
I
island
lyre
pint
quiet
rhyme
sign
style
trial
type
tyke

–y
by
cry
dry
fly
fry
my
ply
pry
shy
sky
sly
spry
spy
sty
try
why

–ies
cries
dies
dries
flies
fries
lies
pies
plies
pries
skies
spies
ties
tries

–ied
cried
died
dried
fried
lied
plied
pried
spied
tied
tried

–ie
die
lie
pie
tie
vie

–uy
buy
guy

–ye
dye
rye

–igh
high
sigh
thigh

–ight
blight
bright
delight
fight
flight
fright
knight
light
might
night
plight
right
sight
slight
tight

Ō

Other:
both
bowl
clothes
comb
goes
loaf
oh
poem
sew
shoulder
soul
though

–obe
globe
lobe
probe
robe
strobe

–ode
code
lode
mode
rode
strode

–ope
cope
dope
grope
hope
lope
mope
pope
rope
scope
slope

–ome
dome
home
Rome

–one
bone
clone
cone
drone
lone
prone
stone
tone

–ole
hole
mole
pole
role
stole
whole

–ote
dote
note
quote
rote
tote
vote
wrote

–oke
broke
choke
coke
joke
poke
smoke
spoke
stoke
stroke
woke
yoke

–ose
chose
close
hose
nose
pose
prose
rose
those

–oad
goad
load
road
toad

–oap
soap

–oam
foam

–oan
groan
Joan
loan
moan

–oal
coal
foal
goal
shoal

–oast
boast
coast
roast
toast

–oat
boat
coat
float
gloat
goat
moat

–oak
cloak
croak
oak
soak

–oze
doze
froze

–o
ago
also
echo
go
hero
no
so

–oe
doe
foe
hoe
Joe
toe
woe

–ow
blow
crow
flow
glow
grow
growth
know
low
mow
row
show
slow
snow
stow
throw

–own
blown
flown
grown
known
own
shown
thrown

below

follow
tomorrow
window
yellow

–old
bold
cold
fold
gold
hold
mold
old
scold
sold
told

–olk
folk
yolk

–olt
bolt
colt
jolt
volt

–oll
knoll
roll
scroll
stroll

–ost
ghost
host
most

			Nouns	Adj.	
at - ate	bid - bide	cod - code	army	angry	steady
can - cane	bit - bite	con - cone	beauty	busy	sticky
cap - cape	dim - dime	cop - cope	body	crazy	sturdy
fad - fade	din - dine	glob - globe	city	deadly	sunny
fat - fate	fin - fine	hop - hope*	company	dirty	tiny
gap - gape	grim - grime	lop - lope*	country	dry	wealthy
glad - glade	grip - gripe*	mop - mope*	cry	dusty	worthy
hat - hate	hid - hide	not - note	dictionary	early	**Verbs**
Jan - Jane	kit - kite	pop - pope	enemy	easy	apply
mad - made	pin - pine*	rob - robe	energy	empty	carry
man - mane	quit - quite	rod - rode	family	friendly	cry
mat - mate	rid - ride	slop - slope	fantasy	funny	defy
nap - nape	rip - ripe	crud - crude	fly	guilty	deny
Nat - Nate	shin - shine	cub - cube	hurry	handy	dry
pan - pane	slid - slide	cut - cute	jury	happy	empty
plan - plane	slim - slime	dud - dude	laboratory	healthy	fly
rag - rage	spin - spine	hug - huge	library	heavy	hurry
rat - rate	spit - spite	plum - plume	memory	hungry	marry
sag - sage	strip - stripe*	tub - tube	mystery	likely	multiply
Sam - same	Tim - time	fed - feed	party	lively	notify
scrap - scrape*	trip - tripe	met - meet	quality	lonely	reply
sham - shame	twin - twine	Ned - need	secretary	lovely	satisfy
slat - slate	win - wine	pep - peep	sky	lucky	study
stag - stage	yip - yipe*	sped - speed	story	pretty	supply
tap - tape*		step - steep	summary	ready	try
van - vane		ten - teen	supply	silly	vary
wag - wage*		wed - weed*	tragedy	sorry	worry

*Both words are verbs.

–ank: bank, blank, clank, crank, drank, Hank, lank, plank, prank, rank, sank, spank, stank, tank, thank, yank

–ang: bang, clang, fang, gang, hang, pang, rang, sang, twang

–eng: length, strength

–ink: blink, brink, chink, clink, drink, ink, kink, link, mink, pink, rink, sink, slink, stink, think, wink

–ing: bring, cling, ding, fling, king, ping, ring, sing, sling, spring, sting, string, swing, thing, wing

–ong: along, gong, long, song, strong, throng, wrong

–onk: bonk, conk, honk

–unk: bunk, chunk, clunk, hunk, junk, plunk, shrunk, skunk, slunk, spunk, stunk, sunk, trunk

–ung: clung, flung, hung, lung, rung, slung, sprung, stung, strung, sung, swung

ng / nk

Other: monk, tongue, young

148

är

Other:
are
guard
heart
hearth
quarrel
starch

–ar
bar
car
char
far
jar
mar
par
scar
spar
star
tar
war

–arb
Barb
barb
garb

–ard
card
chard
hard
lard
reward
shard
ward
yard

–arf
scarf
wharf

–ark
bark
Clark
dark
lark
mark
park
quark
shark
spark
stark

–arl
Carl
Karl
snarl

–arm
arm
charm
farm
harm
swarm
warm

–arn
barn
darn
warn
yarn

–arp
carp
harp
sharp
tarp
warp

–art
art
Bart
cart
chart
dart
mart
part
quart
smart
start
tart
wart

–arve
carve
starve

–arch
march
starch

–arsh
harsh
marsh

–arth
Garth
Martha

–arge
barge
charge
large
Marge

ôr

Other:
coarse
drawer
force
forest
George
gorge
horse
north
source
toward

–or
or
for
nor

–ore
bore
chore
core
gore
lore
more
ore
score
shore
snore
sore
store
swore
tore
wore

–ort
fort
Mort
port
short
snort
sort
sport

–oar
boar
oar
roar
soar

–oard
board
hoard

Other:
prayer
their
there
very
where

–ord
chord
cord
ford
lord
sword

–ork
cork
fork
pork
stork
York

–orm
form
Norm
storm

–orch
porch
scorch
torch

–orth
forth
north

–orn
born
corn
horn
scorn
sworn
thorn
torn
worn

–oor
door
floor
poor

–our
course
court
four
fourth
pour
your

air

–are
bare
care
compare
dare
glare
hare
mare
pare
rare
scare
share
snare
spare
square
stare

–air
air
chair
fair
flair
hair
lair
pair
repair
stair

–ear
bear
pear
swear
tear
wear

–er	–ir	wor	–ur	–ear
her	fir		blur	
per	sir		fur	
	stir		slur	
	whir		spur	
Herb			curb	
verb			disturb	
herd	bird	word	curd	heard
	third		burden	
			surf	
			turf	
clerk	quirk	work	lurk	
jerk	shirk			
perk	smirk			
	girl		burl	pearl
	swirl		curl	
	twirl		hurl	
	whirl			
germ	firm	worm		
term	squirm			
fern			burn	earn
stern			churn	learn
Vern			turn	yearn
	chirp		burp	
			slurp	
terse		worse	curse	hearse
verse			nurse	
			purse	
Bert	dirt		blurt	
Gert	flirt		curt	
pert	shirt		hurt	
	skirt		spurt	
	squirt			
berth	birth	worth		earth
nerve			curve	
serve				
swerve				
perch	birch		church	search
			lurch	
	first	worst	burst	
	thirst			

ʉr

certain	murmur	
circle	occur	
circuit	perceive	
circulate	percent	
circus	perfect	surplus
concern	perform	surprise
courage	perfume	surrender
currency	perhaps	surround
current	permanent	survey
curriculum	permission	survive
curtain	persist	terminate
discourage	person	thermal
durable	plural	thirteen
duration	purchase	thirty
during	purpose	Thursday
early	pursue	turmoil
encourage	pursuit	tourist
endurance	research	version
furnish	return	versus
furniture	rural	vertical
further	search	virgin
jury	servant	virtually
journal	service	virtue
merchant	squirrel	were
mercy	sure	world
merge	surface	worry
murder	surge	worthy

eer

Other:	–eer	–ear
here	beer	appear
weird	career	beard
	cheer	clear
	deer	dear
	engineer	ear
	jeer	fear
	leer	gear
	peer	hear
	pioneer	near
	queer	rear
	sheer	shear
	sneer	smear
	steer	spear
	veer	tear
	volunteer	year

ü

oo
balloon
bloom
boo
boom
boost
boot
booth
brood
broom
choose
cool
coop
doom
drool
droop
food
fool
gloom
goo
goof
goop
goose
groom
hoop
hoot
loom
loon
loop
loose
loot
moo
mood
moon
moose
noon
noose
pooch
poof
pool
proof
roof
room
roost
root
school
scoop
scoot
shoot
smooth
soon
spoon
stool
stoop
swoon
swoop
too
tool
toot
tooth
troop
woo
zoo
zoom

ew
blew
brew
chew
crew
dew
drew
flew
grew
Jew
knew
new
screw
stew
threw

u
flu
duty
Ruth
truth

o
do
to
who

Other:
cruel
group
lose
move
ruin
shoe
soup
through
two
whose

ue
blue
cue
clue
due
glue
sue
true

u-e
crude
dude
dune
flute
June
Luke
plume
prune
rude
rule
spruce
truce
tube
tune

ui
bruise
cruise
fruit
juice
pursuit
recruit
sluice
suit
suitcase

ue
argue
avenue
continue
cruel
issue
rescue
statue
tissue
value

u̇

oo
book
brook
cook
crook
foot
good
hood
hook
look
nook
shook
soot
stood
took
wood
wool

u
bull
full
pull
put

–ould
could
should
would

yü

beauty
cube
cure
cute
few
fuel
fuse
huge
interview
mule
music
pure
review
sure
use
usual
view
viewpoint
you

ou

ou	ow
about	allow
account	bow
amount	brow
around	brown
blouse	browse
bounce	chow
bound	clown
cloud	cow
couch	crowd
count	crown
doubt	down
flour	drown
foul	flower
found	fowl
grouch	frown
ground	gown
hound	growl
hour	how
house	howl
loud	now
louse	owl
mound	plow
mouse	pow
mouth	powder
noun	power
ouch	prow
our	prowl
out	scowl
pouch	shower
pound	towel
pout	tower
proud	town
round	vow
scour	vowel
scout	wow
shout	
slouch	
snout	
sound	
sour	sprout
south	stout
spouse	trout
	wound

oi

–oy
boy
destroy
employ
enjoy
joy
ploy
Roy
royal
soy
toy

–oi
boil
broil
choice
coil
coin
foil
join
joint
noise
oil
point
poise
soil
spoil
toil
voice

Additional Teacher Resources

Step-by-Step Checklist for Getting Started is provided to assist teachers as they plan for the entire year as well as for the first weeks of school.

Why Can't My Child Spell? This article can be reproduced and shared with parents. It gives historical information on spelling and explains some of the reasons children have difficulty learning to spell.

1000 Word Core Spelling List is an alphabetical list of core words that can be reproduced for students and parents.

Weekly Lists can be reproduced and sent home to parents.

Challenge Spelling Lists are examples of the kinds of lists that can be studied by super spellers in the intermediate grades to earn special awards. Tests can be tape-recorded for convenience.

Step-by-Step Checklist for Getting Started

❒ Read the front matter and pages 1–40 of *Spelling Plus*. Highlight key ideas for easy reference. Use this background information when you introduce the program to students.

Pretest Students in September

❒ Read p. 61 for information on pretesting. Although pretesting in September is time-consuming, it is necessary in order to determine where group instruction should begin, especially if students have not come up through the grades with *Spelling Plus*. The words on early lists are much more common and important than those on later lists. Pretesting will help you determine which of these very important words should be reviewed by individuals as well as the group. Use as many of these suggestions for pretesting as are practical within the time constraints you face. Adapt as needed.

❒ Reproduce copies of the test master on pp. 59–60 for pretesting if you teach second grade or higher. First grade teachers begin group instruction with List 1.

❒ Pretest students entering grades 2–6 beginning with Level B. It is best to test in several short sessions.

❒ Check the papers, writing the *correct* spelling of any misspelled word beside it in color.

❒ **Individual lists for review.** Make copies of words each child missed, one for your files, one for parents so that they can help with review, and one for each child's spelling folder as a source of personal words. A photocopy of the actual test the child took, with corrected spellings, will serve.

❒ **Group lists for instruction.** Compile a list of words that several students missed on the pretest for your first group spelling lesson. I make a tally on my test master and include any words that at least five students missed. These words will be "easy" for the other 20+ students, but that's OK. Include your name and the name of your school if you wish on this list of no more than 15 words. Write the list on a copy of p. 32 and use it for your first daily practice activity (see p. 153).

❒ **Determine where group instruction should begin.** Discontinue pretesting when a large number of students are missing a large number of words. Begin group instruction with a list at that level. Generally that will be somewhere between Lists 26 and 36, even for older students. List 35 deals with doubling consonants *(hop – hopping)* and list 36 deals with dropping the silent **e** *(hope – hoping)*. Few students consistently apply these rules without concentrated instruction and extensive review.

Communicate Expectations to Parents

❒ When personal review lists go home, include a letter to parents about spelling and your expectations for homework, copying, first drafts, final drafts, etc. See p. 23 for suggested standards. Include the article on pp. 155–156, the 1000 word list on pp. 157–158, and the weekly lists on pp. 159–160 if you wish. Demonstrate the homework procedure, outlined on p. 156 on Back-to-School Night.

Teach the Daily Practice Activity

❒ Prepare your first group list with review words from the pretests. Write the list on a copy of p. 32. Reproduce this list so that each child gets four identical copies of it on a single sheet of paper. You can begin with review lists and the daily practice activity before pretesting is completed.

❒ Pass out the papers and model the daily practice activity. Follow the directives in the sidebar on p. 30. Make sure students *point to each letter* and *speak very softly* as they practice. The spelling test will be on Friday.

- [ ] If you are working with more than one grade level, you can do the daily practice activity with the whole group, with different students using different lists. In this case, they must speak *very* softly to avoid distracting others. Or, students can simultaneously use recorded lessons for different levels.

Teach the Homework Procedure

- [ ] The next week use the same list to teach the homework procedure. Follow the directions in the sidebar on p. 31. Model this and have students practice until they can do 15 words correctly in about 15 minutes. This shows students that homework need not take long.

Introduce Personal Words

- [ ] When homework and daily practice are in place, introduce personal words. Review pp. 38–40 and decide *if* you want to include personal words at this time. If you do, have students each choose five words they missed on a pretest and copy them in spaces 16–20. Excellent spellers who missed fewer than five words on the pretests fill the five spaces with challenge words. Make sure the words are copied correctly. Allow a few minutes after each daily practice activity for students to practice their personal words, and expect them as a part of the homework.

- [ ] On test day, have students look at their five words to refresh their memories, then put them away and head their test papers. They write their own five personal words in any order first. If they forget what the words were, help them the first week or two but hold them responsible for remembering. Dictate the rest of the test as usual and dictate any five mixed review words if you wish. It's fine if some students also have the teacher-chosen review words as personal words. If they know them, they'll get double credit!

Introduce Dictation

- [ ] The next week, after daily practice is going smoothly, homework is coming in, and personal words are being studied, introduce dictation. See pp. 33–37 for information. Prepare four dictation sentences per day in advance, comprised of words students know. These can be words you've taught or words students knew when pretested. You may use sentences from earlier levels of the *Dictation Resource Book* (see p. 169).

- [ ] Each student heads a sheet of notebook paper to be kept in the spelling folder throughout the week. Dictate the four sentences using the directives in the sidebar of p. 34. The next day, dictate four different sentences, and so on. On Friday, collect and grade the papers, which will each have 20 sentences. See the sidebar on p. 35 for ideas on grading.

- [ ] If you teach more than one age level, try to compose just one set of sentences to use with everyone. It will stretch the younger children, but they can check and fix any mistakes. If the age levels are too far apart, you may need to write separate sentences so that all children are challenged and none are frustrated. Or students may use recorded dictation sentences at their own level.

- [ ] Continue daily dictation throughout the year, gradually introducing and reviewing more and more spelling words, homophones, and language elements listed on p. 37. Dictation sentences can be lifted directly from students' creative writing. Take your cues for what needs to be included in dictation from student writing. If you notice mistakes on a language skill you've already taught, review and reteach the skill through dictation. Review the rules of capitalization, punctuation and grammar again and again and ask students to apply them in dictation sentences until the rules are *mastered*. Students must recall and recite the rules as requested by the teacher during dictation.

154

Review Testing

❑ Review must be a continuous and integral part of a good spelling program. If time allows, dictate five mixed review words after each daily practice activity, to fill the last five lines of the worksheet.

❑ Add five mixed review words to each weekly test. If certain words are "demons" for several students, test them week after week. Students should know they are accountable *forever* for spelling these words correctly.

❑ Periodically, perhaps on a short week such as Thanksgiving week, do a major review test. Duplicate pp. 59–60 and dictate any or all words taught so far, including words several students missed on the pretest. Check review tests as you did the pretests, add misspelled words to personal word lists, and perhaps compile a review list of words several students missed. Don't be discouraged if there are more mistakes than you'd like to see. If students have been misspelling a word for years, it may take a long time to relearn it correctly, but patience will eventually pay off.

❑ At the end of the school year, do as complete a review test as you can manage, beginning with recently-taught words. If time allows, test all earlier lists from *Spelling Plus*. Students can compare their results with the pretest they took in September.

Weekly Planning Checklist for Spelling Once Everything Is "On Line"

❑ Prepare and reproduce a group list. Each student needs one sheet with four identical lists and one half sheet with a list to take home. Use one of the lists in *Spelling Plus* or one you compiled. See p. 32 for more.

❑ Write dictation sentences, preferably four for each day. Use *all* words from the previous week's spelling list the following week, plus at least a few sets of homophones each day. Review language elements (p. 37) you've already taught and introduce no more than

one new element a week, including it in all or nearly all sentences during the week. Don't introduce another new element until all or nearly all students show a firm grasp of the last one. Contractions should be mastered, before possessives are introduced, for example, to prevent confusion.

❑ Throughout the week, collect personal words, from last week's spelling tests, dictation papers, creative writing, journals, etc. Refer to p. 39 for ideas on how to manage this.

❑ On Monday, pass out the weekly worksheet for the daily practice activity, the list to go home, and the personal words, from which students select five. Every child needs five personal words. Good spellers may fill in with challenge words or vocabulary words.

❑ Each day do the daily practice activity and daily dictation with the group. On Tuesdays through Fridays, collect homework papers and scan them. If any students are misspelling words in homework, address the problem. Wrong practice is harmful! Acknowledge students who diligently and carefully check their homework.

Teach Dictionary Skills

❑ With a class set of identical dictionaries, take ten minutes or so a day with the group for a few weeks to help all students learn to locate 10 words within 10 minutes in the dictionary:
– Survey the entire dictionary.
– Locate the section with any beginning letter the teacher dictates or writes on the board.
– Locate the page number for any guide word the teacher dictates or writes on the board.
– Locate any word on a given page.
– Locate any entry word the teacher writes.
– Locate 10 words in 10 minutes. Using a reproduced list of 10 entry words, students locate the words and note each page number and column number (1 or 2), aiming to finish within 10 minutes. Repeat this activity day after day with different lists until all or nearly all students have met this mastery standard.

Why Can't My Child Spell?

Any child who finds spelling easy and spells well in writing has been blessed with a talent that few children possess. The best spellers have excellent visual memory. As one student put it, they "snap a picture of the word" with their minds, and refer to that mental image as they write or proofread.

If spelling is difficult for your child, he/she is not alone! Even brilliant people may have trouble with spelling. Spelling ability is more of a talent than an indication of intelligence. President Andrew Jackson once blurted out in frustration: "It's a poor mind that can think of only one way to spell a word!"

Our system of spelling is extremely complex and inconsistent. Sounds can be spelled in several ways, letters can represent several sounds, and most spelling "rules" have many exceptions! It's no wonder children have difficulty learning to spell.

The roots of the problem are fascinating, and lie deep in the history of the English language. Here are a few highlights:

- English speakers throughout history have freely borrowed words from dozens of languages. To show the origin of these words, English kept the original spellings. All words with **ph**, for example, are from Greek.
- English was spoken long before it was written. The Latin alphabet, which was adopted for writing English, didn't fit. It had fewer letters than English had sounds.
- Originally, words were spelled the way they were pronounced. Because of the dozens of dialects in England, there were dozens of pronunciations, and so dozens of acceptable spellings for most words.
- In Shakespeare's day, creative spelling was considered a mark of genius. More than 80 spellings of his name have been found!
- The first printers spelled words in various ways in order to justify their lines of type. Silent e's were added or deleted, and consonants were doubled or not depending on printer preference and spacing.
- Pronunciation has changed drastically over the centuries, while spelling has stayed the same. 400 years ago, the now silent letters in *write*, *knife* and *comb* were pronounced. The **gh** in *light* had a guttural sound no longer used in English. *Name* had two syllables. *Bird* sounded like *beard*, and *daughter* rhymed with *laughter!*
- Samuel Johnson compiled the first English dictionary in 1755. In order to alphabetize words, he had to choose a preferred spelling. He was not consistent in all cases *(downhil – uphill)*, but his dictionary was accepted as the final authority on spelling for some 100 years. Noah Webster reformed some spellings in his American dictionary, but public outcry and reverence for tradition prevented him from making too many changes.

"The present bad spelling is only bad, because contrary to the present bad rules; under new rules it would be good. The difficulty of learning to spell well in the old way is so great, that few attain it, thousands and thousands writing on to old age without ever being able to acquire it."
— *Benjamin Franklin*

Many historical figures have advocated spelling reform. Benjamin Franklin even developed a whole new alphabet, with as many letters as English has sounds! But spelling was not reformed, despite the effort and financial support of eminent people such as Benjamin Franklin, Noah Webster, Andrew Carnegie, Theodore Roosevelt and George Bernard Shaw. So we're stuck with an illogical and complicated system of spelling that frustrates adults as well as students.

Learning to spell correctly is not easy for most, but it is important for all, especially with increased competition for good jobs. Even general readers make judgments about a person's intelligence and level of education based on spelling. Poor spelling on a resume can offend an employer and cost an otherwise qualified candidate a job!

The idea that spelling is an indicator of intelligence and a good education comes from the British class system. Historically in England, only the children of the well-to-do could afford to go to school and learn to write and spell. People who couldn't spell were considered lower class and uneducated. Upper class children with little talent for spelling were publicly shamed for their mistakes, so they were *powerfully* motivated to study! Spelling bees are a holdover of these old traditions.

Children have the best chance of learning to spell well if parents and teachers share common, reasonable expectations and goals. A child needs every possible ally in the difficult task of learning to spell in English.

Our Queer Language

When the English tongue we speak
    Why is **break** not rhymed with **freak**?
Will you tell me why it's true
    We say **sew** but likewise **few**?
And the maker of a verse
    Cannot cap his **horse** with **worse**.
Beard sounds not the same as **heard**;
    Cord is different from **word**.
Cow is **cow** but low is **low**,
    Shoe is never rhymed with **foe**.
Think of **hose** and **dose** and **lose**,
    And think of **goose** and not of **choose**.
Think of **comb** and **tomb** and **bomb**,
    Doll and **roll**, **home** and **some**.
And since **pay** is rhymed with **say**,
    Why not **paid** with **said**, I pray?
We have **blood** and **food** and **good**;
    Mould is not pronounced like **could**.
Wherefore **done** but **gone** and **lone**?
    Is there any reason known?
And, in short, it seems to me
    Sounds and letters disagree.
Evelyn Baring, Lord Cromer
Spectator, Aug. 9, 1902

What Is a Successful Speller?

Given that not everyone has the talent to become an excellent speller, and that spelling is important in our society, what does it take to become an adequate and successful speller? Successful spellers:

- *Accept personal responsibility for correct spelling in their own writing. Children must know that spelling is important and care about getting it right.*
- *Master the most common and useful words and rules. Amazingly, 90% of text in English consists of only 1000 base words, and a large percentage of common misspellings are of relatively few words.*
- *Use an adequate and systematic method for memorizing new spellings.*
- *Independently use the dictionary and other memory aids.*
- *Recognize regular and irregular spellings.*
- *Understand how words are constructed (roots, prefixes and suffixes).*

Do's and Don'ts for Concerned Parents

- **Don't** equate spelling ability with intelligence, quality of education, or personal worth. If your child isn't talented in spelling, learn what his/her talents are and foster them.
- **Do** emphasize the value and importance of correct spelling without losing perspective. Spelling is to writing as appearance is to character. Good appearance counts, as does good spelling. But a person's *ideas, values* and *character* are far more important.
- **Do** hold up high standards while acknowledging the difficulty of the child's task. Have confidence in his/her ability to learn. Encourage, be patient and consistent. Reward progress without expecting perfection.
- **Don't** expect good spelling in first draft writing, or point out spelling errors in a child's writing before you have read and responded to the message. It is difficult if not impossible for children to concentrate on spelling at the same time as they concentrate on the ideas they are trying to express in writing. Eventually, most common spellings should be *mastered* so that they require little or no conscious thought and *are* correct in first drafts.
- **Do** expect good spelling in final draft writing, and expect children to copy spellings accurately.
- **Don't** expect a child to remember a spelling word just because it's been studied on a list and spelled right on a weekly test. An *incredible* amount of review and practice may be needed for mastery.
- **Don't** blame teachers for a child's problems with spelling or expect spelling to be learned *only* at school. Cooperation between teachers and parents is crucial.

How Can Parents Help with Spelling?

- **Do** make sure your child does homework and practices spelling each night. Provide a special, quiet place, with enough light, a good chair, a desk or table, and a clock. Have materials such as paper, pencils and reference books gathered and kept together in a desk, drawer or box.
- **Do** set aside a special time to do homework, with the TV and radio off. Make homework a priority in the family.
- **Do** get your child a dictionary appropriate for his age level. Teach and reteach him how to look up words. Pay attention and encourage him whenever he uses it without assistance.
- **Don't** *always* refer children to the dictionary for spellings or they could see it as a hated chore.
- **Do** place as much responsibility as possible on the child when you're asked for a spelling. Have him list some possible spellings and you confirm which is correct. Or have him suggest letters and you fill in the letters not known.
- **Do** proofread your child's final draft papers after he has edited them to make sure that all mistakes were caught. Rather than point out specific mistakes, first indicate that there is a mistake on a line, and challenge the child to find it and fix it.
- **Do** consider keeping a record of words your child misspells in his/her writing, perhaps a 3x5 card file with a card for each word in alphabetical order, or a personal dictionary with a page for words beginning with each letter. The child can use this rather than the big dictionary for words already looked up once. You can spend a few minutes each day helping your child review and practice some of these words. Whenever they are spelled correctly in writing, **celebrate!**

Regardless of your child's spelling talent, he/she *can* become a successful speller. Maintain high standards, focus on the positive, celebrate every success, and be very patient!

Susan C. Anthony is an award-winning author and teacher. ***Spelling Plus: 1000 Words toward Spelling Success,*** *from which this article was taken, is available from Nature's Workshop Plus, P.O. Box 425, Danville, IN 46122 www.workshopplus.com, www.SusanCAnthony.com*

Spelling Homework Procedure

1. *Read the word aloud from the spelling list.*
2. *Spell the word aloud as you point to each letter, then read it.*
3. *Write the word on your own paper as you spell and read it.*
4. *Check the model. Point to each letter.*
5. *Check and correct the word you wrote. Point to each letter.*
6. *Cover the first word you wrote. Repeat steps 3–5 two more times.*
7. *Close your eyes. Spell the word aloud and say it.*

The final result is a paper with each word written perfectly three times. If all steps were done correctly, the learner has practiced each word 11 times in 50–60 seconds. Only three of the practices were written.

1000 Word Core Spelling List

Number indicates the list on which the word is introduced in Spelling Plus.

4 a	4 and	41 because	8 clock	60 definitely
52 a lot	28 animal	24 become	14 close	69 delicious
54 able	25 another	15 been	49 clothes	64 describe
17 about	53 answer	41 before	20 cold	64 description
14 above	21 any	29 began	66 college	51 destroy
57 absent	37 anybody	29 begin	14 come	59 develop
59 accept	37 anyway	35 beginning	36 coming	59 development
63 accident	67 apologize	19 being	66 commit	6 did
63 accidentally	67 apology	33 believe	65 committee	22 didn't
65 accommodate	65 appear	31 below	60 complete	33 die
54 ache	67 appearance	61 benefit	60 completely	33 died
66 achieve	69 appreciate	5 best	64 concentrate	61 difference
67 acquaint	65 approach	34 better	69 conscience	61 different
67 acquaintance	52 April	41 between	69 conscious	63 difficult
46 across	55 arctic	57 bicycle	64 continue	36 dining
24 act	6 are	6 big	69 continuous	34 dinner
58 action	66 area	29 bird	66 control	58 direction
60 actual	22 aren't	8 black	61 convenient	29 dirty
60 actually	55 argue	33 blew	30 copy	65 disappear
58 addition	57 argument	53 blood	38 corner	65 disappoint
46 address	16 arm	31 blow	7 cost	69 discipline
64 affect	17 around	18 blue	21 could	68 discuss
32 afraid	16 art	38 board	47 countries	68 discussion
24 after	54 article	30 body	45 country	63 disease
30 afternoon	4 as	18 book	42 course	67 distance
32 again	4 ask	20 both	50 cousin	10 do
32 against	19 asked	34 bottom	38 cover	57 doctor
11 age	1 at	41 bought	47 cries	19 does
32 air	11 ate	18 boy	67 criticism	22 doesn't
9 all	58 attention	39 bread	67 criticize	7 dog
52 all right	52 August	34 break	10 cry	19 doing
29 allow	50 aunt	34 breakfast	19 crying	58 dollar
46 almost	57 author	54 bridge	7 cut	22 don't
46 alone	13 away	67 brilliant	16 dark	14 done
26 along	38 awful	26 bring	50 daughter	53 doubt
46 already	23 awhile	14 broke	13 day	24 down
46 although	8 back	50 brother	39 dead	24 draw
46 always	55 barely	41 brought	26 dear	7 drop
1 am	10 be	29 brown	39 death	35 dropped
40 America	30 bear	56 build	62 deceive	35 dropping
40 American	47 beautiful	56 building	52 December	43 during
20 among	45 beauty	56 built	68 decide	51 duty
1 an	24 became	47 business	68 decided	27 each
			68 decision	47 earlier
			15 deep	49 early
			60 definite	39 earth

47 easiest	32 fair	9 gave	39 head	61 independent
27 east	67 familiar	60 generally	26 hear	63 innocent
27 easy	47 families	5 get	39 heard	25 inside
27 eat	45 family	35 getting	33 heart	39 instead
54 edge	16 far	29 girl	39 heavy	61 intelligent
64 education	69 fascinate	9 give	62 height	57 interest
64 effect	53 fasten	36 giving	18 hello	57 interesting
62 eight	50 father	10 go	5 help	25 into
62 either	44 favorite	19 goes	16 her	6 is
49 eleven	52 February	19 going	13 here	56 island
48 else	15 feel	14 gone	40 high	2 it
65 embarrass	19 feeling	18 good	6 him	22 it's
5 end	5 felt	18 goodbye	25 himself	22 its
45 enemy	33 few	3 got	6 his	25 itself
51 enjoy	33 field	34 gotten	14 home	52 January
41 enough	40 fight	59 government	14 hope	69 jealous
49 entertain	58 figure	35 grabbed	36 hoping	66 journal
66 equipped	9 fill	11 grade	35 hopping	52 July
63 escape	19 filled	62 grammar	17 horse	52 June
55 especially	55 final	50 grandfather	51 hospital	7 just
56 etc.	55 finally	50 grandma	7 hot	15 keep
18 even	20 find	13 gray	17 hour	5 kept
18 evening	12 fire	34 great	17 house	56 key
21 ever	29 first	15 green	29 how	20 kind
21 every	9 five	17 ground	29 however	33 knew
37 everyone	10 fly	41 group	49 humorous	31 know
37 everything	31 follow	31 grow	49 hundred	54 knowledge
37 everywhere	30 food	63 guarantee	45 hungry	32 known
65 exaggerate	18 foot	56 guard	47 hurried	32 laid
59 example	17 for	56 guess	45 hurry	56 language
59 excellent	54 force	56 guilty	46 hurrying	16 large
59 except	42 foreign	57 gym	43 hurt	4 last
59 excite	51 forest	4 had	2 I	38 later
59 excitement	25 forget	32 hair	22 I'll	42 laugh
59 exciting	49 forty	53 half	22 I'm	42 laughed
59 excuse	17 found	4 hand	48 idea	42 laughter
59 exercise	21 four	42 handwriting	64 identify	13 lay
61 existence	42 fourth	34 happen	2 if	28 lead
59 expect	15 free	34 happened	64 imagine	28 leader
59 experience	43 Friday	47 happiness	60 immediate	39 learn
59 explain	41 friend	45 happy	60 immediately	39 learned
60 extremely	20 from	16 hard	44 important	27 least
30 eye	20 front	4 has	54 impossible	27 leave
11 face	9 full	9 have	2 in	5 led
24 fact	43 further	22 haven't	63 incident	62 leisure
32 fail	11 game	10 he	61 independence	26 length

158

8 less
46 lesson
5 let
53 let's
22 library
52 library
33 lie
44 life
5 light
40 lightning
12 like
36 liked
6 line
53 list
23 listen
61 listened
37 little
36 live
56 lived
20 living
23 lonely
46 long
26 look
18 looked
23 loose
19 lose
7 lot
14 love
31 low
8 luck
7 luckily
45 lucky
66 machine
11 made
61 magazine
32 main
11 make
36 making
4 man
21 many
52 March
34 matter
13 may
52 May
25 maybe
10 me
28 mean

28 meant
50 measure
53 medicine
15 meet
5 men
44 middle
40 might
12 mile
49 million
17 mind
48 minute
3 miss
69 mischievous
51 misspell
14 modern
37 Monday
43 money
48 month
52 moon
29 moon
48 more
48 morning
67 most
48 mother
44 motor
68 mountain
7 move
13 moving
51 Mr.
10 Ms.
57 much
3 music
20 must
27 my

32 name
65 national
50 near
40 necessary
12 need
16 neighbor
48 neither
41 nephew
63 nervous
66 never
8 new
57 next
13 nice
12 nickel
65 niece
50 night
40 parents
62 neither
48 niece
16 nine
49 nineteen
12 ninety
37 no
10 nobody
51 noise
48 noisy
67 north
48 northern
44 not
68 note
44 nothing
35 notice
7 November
51 now
55 October
30 of
12 off
21 office
6 often
21 oh
44 old
26 on
26 once
29 one
6 only
22 open
13 opinion
6 opinion
29 opportunity
38 opposite
46 or
23 other
26 our
29 out
38 outside
23 over
46 own
38 page

12 paid
43 parallel
62 parents
54 part
40 particular
8 pass
41 passed
56 patient
66 pattern
8 pay
63 peculiar
68 people
44 perfect
44 perform
68 perhaps
63 period
38 person
55 physical
44 picture
35 pie
7 piece
51 place
55 plain
6 plan
63 planned
54 planning
30 play
56 played
63 playing
54 pleasant
47 please
62 pocket
15 poem
58 point
62 poison
46 poor
15 possess
15 possible
30 power
45 practical
37 practically
37 secret
17 practice
45 prairie
50 prepare
56 prettier
21 pretty

63 price
31 principal
18 principle
8 prison
12 private
54 privilege
56 probably
54 problem
63 procedure
56 profession
44 professor
55 program
44 progress
51 promise
35 pronunciation
7 purpose
55 put
9 question
63 quick
12 quiet
8 quit
63 quite
40 rain
54 raise
56 reach
66 read
63 ready
44 real
51 realize
21 really
35 reason
44 receipt
11 receive
43 recess
64 recognize
43 recommend
25 red
11 reference
46 referred
13 regular
55 relative
50 relief
57 remember
15 repeat
30 repetition
12 responsible

21 restaurant
31 return
18 rhythm
54 ridge
12 right
56 road
63 room
54 rules
55 run
26 running
29 safety
26 said
37 sale
6 same
21 sandwich
12 saw
6 say
13 scare
35 scared
31 scene
46 school
12 science
30 scissors
9 sea
34 search
29 second
41 season
6 see
47 seem
44 seen
68 seize
49 sense
15 sentence
33 separate
15 September
51 serious
51 seven
37 several
28 shall
15 she
11 shine
16 shining
27 short

9 should
54 show
18 shown
7 sick
12 side
35 sign
5 similar
25 simple
18 since
54 sincerely
56 single
63 sister
57 sit
13 six
47 size
22 skiing
13 sledding
6 sleep
45 slipped
13 slow
22 small
26 smile
55 smooth
13 so
30 social
31 some
20 somebody
57 something
41 sometimes
33 somewhere
29 son
14 soon
41 sorry
41 south
41 speak
41 special
18 speech
13 spring
20 stairs
51 stand
25 start
36 state
16 statement
16 stay
10 stayed
57 stepped

22 still
54 stomach
18 stood
7 stop
5 stopped
25 stopping
21 stories
49 story
43 straight
6 street
13 strength
29 strong
38 student
46 studied
23 study
23 studying
23 success
23 succeed
23 such
24 sudden
50 sugar
24 suggest
24 summary
44 summer
25 Sunday
38 upon
9 suppose
38 supposed to
36 sure
6 surprise
25 surprised
60 swimming
55 system

9 table
22 take
22 taking
22 talk
57 taught
38 teach
50 teacher
24 team
23 tell
23 terrible
23 than
23 thank you
23 that
22 that's
43 the
49 their
23 them
23 themselves
21 then
57 there
38 these
50 they
24 they're
23 type
23 thing
23 think
46 third
40 this
25 those
23 though
23 thought
23 thousand
38 three
46 threw
38 through
6 throw
36 Thursday
60 ticket
36 tie
6 tight
25 time
60 tired
55 to
12 today
7 together
38 told
9 tomorrow
12 too
38 took
9 touch
12 tough
23 toward
38 town
44 tragedy
25 tried
18 trouble
44 truly
9 true
57 try
19 trying

22 Tuesday
23 turn
23 twelve
23 twenty-one
23 two
57 tying
38 type
50 uncle
24 under
23 understand
23 United States
23 unless
23 until
46 up
38 upon
9 us
38 use
38 used to
36 using
6 usual
25 usually
60 very
55 view
55 voice
38 wait
38 waiting
38 walk
24 want
24 war
42 warm
42 was
42 watch
42 water
21 way
16 we
31 weak
14 wear
7 weather
25 week
6 Wednesday
9 weight
12 weird
43 welcome
18 well
44 went
9 were

43 weren't
43 what
43 when
43 where
43 whether
43 which
43 while
43 white
43 who
43 who's
43 whole
43 whose
43 why
12 wide
23 will
31 win
38 window
6 winter
6 wish
21 with
25 without
55 woman
55 women
38 wonder
38 wonderful
24 word
24 work
24 world
21 would
42 wreck
42 write
42 writer
42 writing
42 written
42 wrong
42 wrote
31 yellow
38 yes
15 yesterday
22 you
8 you're
41 young
41 your
8 (your city)
40 (your state)

List 1
1. am
2. an
3. at

List 2
1. I
2. if
3. in
4. it

List 3
1. on
2. not
3. got

List 4
1. and
2. can
3. plan
4. hand
5. stand
6. man
7. than
8. that
9. last
10. as
11. ask
12. had
13. has
14. was
15. a

List 5
1. let
2. get
3. yes
4. red
5. led
6. men
7. end
8. went
9. then
10. them
11. best
12. felt
13. help
14. next
15. kept

List 6
1. is
2. his
3. him
4. big
5. did
6. win
7. sit
8. quit
9. wish
10. with
11. list
12. this
13. the
14. they
15. are

List 7
1. hot
2. lot
3. dog
4. cost
5. stop
6. drop
7. us
8. up
9. but
10. cut
11. run
12. just
13. must
14. much
15. such

List 8
1. back
2. black
3. check
4. sick
5. clock
6. luck
7. quick
8. off
9. class
10. pass
11. less
12. miss
13. you
14. your
15. our

List 9
1. all
2. call
3. small
4. well
5. tell
6. fill
7. will
8. still
9. full
10. have
11. gave
12. give
13. live
14. five
15. move

List 10
1. go
2. no
3. so
4. do
5. to
6. be
7. he
8. me
9. we
10. she
11. by
12. my
13. try
14. cry
15. fly

List 11
1. came
2. same
3. name
4. game
5. ate
6. state
7. age
8. page
9. take
10. make
11. made
12. grade
13. sale
14. face
15. place

List 12
1. time
2. nine
3. line
4. shine
5. nice
6. price
7. life
8. quite
9. like
10. mile
11. smile
12. fire
13. wide
14. side
15. size

List 13
1. day
2. may
3. pay
4. lay
5. way
6. away
7. gray
8. play
9. stay
10. say
11. said
12. were
13. here
14. there
15. these

List 14
1. home
2. hope
3. note
4. chose
5. close
6. those
7. broke
8. love
9. above
10. some
11. come
12. one
13. done
14. gone
15. use

List 15
1. free
2. three
3. see
4. seem
5. seen
6. green
7. deep
8. sleep
9. keep
10. street
11. meet
12. week
13. feel
14. need
15. been

List 16
1. car
2. far
3. dark
4. hard
5. arm
6. warm
7. war
8. art
9. part
10. start
11. large
12. talk
13. walk
14. want
15. her

List 17
1. or
2. for
3. north
4. short
5. horse
6. house
7. out
8. about
9. around
10. found
11. ground
12. south
13. hour
14. oh
15. of

List 18
1. took
2. look
3. book
4. stood
5. foot
6. good
7. goodbye
8. hello
9. even
10. evening
11. morning
12. blue
13. true
14. boy
15. their

List 19
1. asked
2. called
3. looked
4. played
5. stayed
6. filled
7. doing
8. going
9. playing
10. trying
11. crying
12. being
13. feeling
14. goes
15. does

List 20
1. old
2. cold
3. told
4. both
5. most
6. find
7. mind
8. kind
9. child
10. second
11. month
12. among
13. front
14. from
15. other

List 21
1. once
2. four
3. two
4. six
5. seven
6. any
7. many
8. never
9. ever
10. every
11. very
12. would
13. could
14. should
15. shall

List 22
1. its
2. it's
3. that's
4. let's
5. I'll
6. I'm
7. they're
8. you're
9. can't
10. don't
11. didn't
12. doesn't
13. aren't
14. weren't
15. haven't

List 23
1. who
2. who's
3. whose
4. lose
5. why
6. what
7. when
8. where
9. which
10. whether
11. white
12. while
13. awhile
14. whole
15. more

List 24
1. act
2. fact
3. saw
4. draw
5. work
6. word
7. world
8. only
9. open
10. over
11. under
12. after
13. become
14. became
15. welcome

List 25
1. itself
2. himself
3. themselves
4. into
5. upon
6. forget
7. maybe
8. cannot
9. today
10. inside
11. outside
12. without
13. understand
14. another
15. put

List 26
1. along
2. long
3. length
4. strong
5. strength
6. spring
7. bring
8. thing
9. think
10. thank you
11. year
12. near
13. hear
14. dear
15. clear

List 27
1. weak
2. speak
3. each
4. reach
5. teach
6. teacher
7. eat
8. cheat
9. easy
10. east
11. least
12. please
13. leave
14. real
15. really

List 28
1. sea
2. season
3. reason
4. lead
5. leader
6. clean
7. team
8. mean
9. meant
10. read
11. ready
12. case
13. care
14. scare
15. animal

List 29
1. now
2. how
3. however
4. down
5. brown
6. town
7. allow
8. power
9. dirty
10. bird
11. girl
12. third
13. first
14. begin
15. began

List 30
1. too
2. loose
3. food
4. moon
5. soon
6. room
7. smooth
8. school
9. afternoon
10. choose
11. eye
12. body
13. copy
14. wear
15. bear

List 31
1. own
2. know
3. known
4. show
5. shown
6. blow
7. slow
8. grow
9. throw
10. low
11. below
12. follow
13. yellow
14. window
15. tomorrow

List 32
1. wait
2. waiting
3. rain
4. plain
5. main
6. paid
7. laid
8. fail
9. again
10. against
11. afraid
12. air
13. fair
14. hair
15. raise

List 33
1. new
2. knew
3. few
4. blew
5. threw
6. view
7. die
8. died
9. lie
10. believe
11. pie
12. piece
13. field
14. chief
15. heart

List 34
1. better
2. matter
3. gotten
4. dinner
5. summer
6. sudden
7. happen
8. happened
9. suppose
10. supposed to
11. bottom
12. great
13. break
14. breakfast
15. quiet

List 35
1. stepped
2. slipped
3. grabbed
4. planned
5. planning
6. dropped
7. dropping
8. stopped
9. stopping
10. hopping
11. getting
12. running
13. sledding
14. swimming
15. beginning

List 36
1. tired
2. scared
3. liked
4. lived
5. used to
6. using
7. shining
8. dining
9. taking
10. making
11. moving
12. giving
13. living
14. hoping
15. coming

List 37
1. nobody
2. nothing
3. anyway
4. anybody
5. everyone
6. everything
7. everywhere
8. somebody
9. something
10. somewhere
11. sometimes
12. catch
13. watch
14. stretch
15. little

List 38
1. cover
2. later
3. center
4. corner
5. water
6. winter
7. wonder
8. wonderful
9. careful
10. awful
11. until
12. yesterday
13. type
14. road
15. board

List 39
1. weather
2. measure
3. heavy
4. head
5. bread
6. dead
7. death
8. instead
9. pleasant
10. search
11. heard
12. early
13. earth
14. learn
15. learned

List 40
1. fight
2. light
3. might
4. night
5. right
6. tight
7. high
8. tough
9. enough
10. though
11. through
12. thought
13. young
14. group
15. friend

List 41
1. write
2. writer
3. writing
4. handwriting
5. wrote
6. wrong
7. wreck
8. written
9. laugh
10. laughed
11. laughter
12. caught
13. taught
14. course
15. fourth

List 42
1. bought
2. brought
3. before
4. because
5. between
6. private
7. sugar
8. sure
9. during
10. purpose
11. program
12. problem
13. promise
14. return
15. important

List 43
1. surprise
2. surprised
3. remember
4. terrible
5. trouble
6. favorite
7. chocolate
8. single
9. busy
10. study
11. sorry
12. hungry
13. lonely
14. country
15. lucky

List 44
1. circle
2. city
3. story
4. people
5. middle
6. enemy
7. hungry
8. lonely
9. country
10. lucky
11. study
12. sorry
13. carry
14. family
15. beauty

List 45
1. always
2. almost
3. already
4. although
5. alone
6. across
7. unless
8. recess
9. address
10. lesson
11. busy
12. single
13. favorite
14. beautiful
15. business

List 46
1. carefully
2. lesson
3. luckily
4. happiness
5. carrying
6. hurrying
7. studying
8. tried
9. hurried
10. carried
11. studied
12. earlier
13. prettier
14. easiest
15. business

List 47
1. cries
2. countries
3. families
4. stories
5. tried
6. hurried
7. carried
8. studied
9. earlier
10. prettier
11. easiest
12. luckily
13. happiness
14. business
15. beautiful

List 48
1. noise
2. noisy
3. point
4. voice
5. poison
6. prison
7. person
8. period
9. perhaps
10. perfect
11. else
12. idea
13. office
14. notice
15. practice

List 49
1. mountain
2. captain
3. certain
4. entertain
5. grandfather
6. eleven
7. twelve
8. twenty-one
9. forty
10. nineteen
11. ninety
12. hundred
13. thousand
14. million
15. relative

List 50
1. sister
2. mother
3. brother
4. father
5. grandma
6. daughter
7. son
8. parents
9. uncle
10. aunt
11. cousin
12. niece
13. nephew
14. secret
15. secretary

List 51
1. stairs
2. prairie
3. duty
4. rules
5. minute
6. hospital
7. enjoy
8. destroy
9. together
10. forest
11. library
12. modern
13. northern
14. pattern
15. central

List 52
1. sentence
2. often
3. fasten
4. listen
5. listened
6. climb
7. climbed
8. climbing
9. answer
10. doubt
11. simple
12. table
13. able
14. possible
15. impossible

List 53
1. social
2. special
3. article
4. since
5. especially
6. sincerely
7. knowledge
8. final
9. finally
10. build
11. built
12. building
13. guess
14. guard
15. guilty

List 54
1. ridge
2. bridge
3. edge
4. stomach
5. ache
6. character
7. arctic
8. argue
9. statement
10. safety
11. barely
12. poor
13. blood
14. tragedy
15. medicine

List 55
1. woman
2. women
3. children
4. probably
5. language
6. several
7. toward
8. guess
9. guard
10. guilty
11. built
12. build
13. building
14. interest
15. interesting

List 56
1. tie
2. tying
3. author
4. motor
5. doctor
6. argument
7. truly
8. sincerely
9. skiing
10. passed
11. straight
12. absent
13. gym
14. bicycle
15. etc.

List 57
1. sense
2. pocket
3. ticket
4. nickel
5. figure
6. picture
7. speech
8. regular
9. dollar
10. calendar
11. question
12. direction
13. action
14. addition
15. attention

List 58
1. several
2. toward
3. author
4. motor
5. doctor
6. argument
7. truly
8. interest
9. interesting
10. skiing
11. passed
12. straight
13. absent
14. gym
15. bicycle

List 59
1. accept
2. except
3. excellent
4. excuse
5. excite
6. exciting
7. excitement
8. example
9. exercise
10. experience
11. explain
12. expect
13. develop
14. development
15. government

List 60
1. carefully
2. complete
3. completely
4. extremely
5. definite
6. definitely
7. actual
8. actually
9. usual
10. usually
11. practical
12. practically
13. generally
14. immediate
15. immediately

List 61
1. music
2. misspell
3. magazine
4. lightning
5. opinion
6. benefit
7. different
8. difference
9. deceive
10. receive
11. receipt
12. seize
13. weird
14. foreign
15. rhythm

List 62
1. eight
2. weight
3. height
4. neighbor
5. leisure
6. either
7. neither
8. guarantee
9. disappoint
10. concentrate
11. exaggerate
12. education
13. procedure
14. a lot
15. all right

List 63
1. incident
2. accident
3. accidentally
4. escape
5. innocent
6. difficult
7. continue
8. imagine
9. appear
10. disappear
11. recommend
12. necessary
13. suggest
14. prepare
15. commit

List 64
1. affect
2. effect
3. ache
4. control
5. relief
6. realize
7. achieve
8. apologize
9. recognize
10. criticize
11. criticism
12. opportunity
13. privilege
14. approach
15. college

List 65
1. approach
2. opportunity
3. privilege
4. achieve
5. realize
6. control
7. relief
8. describe
9. description
10. embarrass
11. committee
12. accommodate
13. responsible
14. separate
15. national

List 66
1. college
2. apology
3. apologize
4. physical
5. decide
6. decided
7. recognize
8. criticize
9. criticism
10. occasion
11. occur
12. occurred
13. occurring
14. occurrence
15. acquaintance

List 67
1. summary
2. principle
3. physical
4. decide
5. decided
6. criticize
7. criticism
8. occasion
9. success
10. succeed
11. profession
12. professor
13. possess
14. discuss
15. discussion

List 68
1. principle
2. principal
3. physical
4. decide
5. decided
6. recognize
7. criticize
8. criticism
9. occasion
10. acquaint
11. acquaintance
12. appearance
13. possess
14. brilliant
15. familiar

List 69
1. scene
2. fascinate
3. discipline
4. scissors
5. science
6. conscience
7. conscious
8. nervous
9. jealous
10. serious
11. humorous
12. continuous
13. mischievous
14. delicious
15. appreciate

161

States 1

1. Maine (ME)
2. Vermont (VT)
3. New Hampshire (NH)
4. Massachusetts (MA)
5. Connecticut (CT)
6. Rhode Island (RI)
7. New York (NY)
8. Pennsylvania (PA)
9. New Jersey (NJ)
10. Delaware (DE)
11. Maryland (MD)
12. Virginia (VA)
13. West Virginia (WV)
14. North Carolina (NC)
15. South Carolina (SC)
16. Kentucky (KY)
17. Tennessee (TN)
18. Mississippi (MS)
19. Alabama (AL)
20. Georgia (GA)
21. Florida (FL)
22. Arkansas (AR)
23. Louisiana (LA)
24. Oklahoma (OK)
25. Texas (TX)

States 2

1. Alaska (AK)
2. Hawaii (HI)
3. Washington (WA)
4. Oregon (OR)
5. California (CA)
6. Nevada (NV)
7. Idaho (ID)
8. Montana (MT)
9. Wyoming (WY)
10. Utah (UT)
11. Colorado (CO)
12. Arizona (AZ)
13. New Mexico (NM)
14. North Dakota (ND)
15. South Dakota (SD)
16. Nebraska (NE)
17. Kansas (KS)
18. Minnesota (MN)
19. Iowa (IA)
20. Missouri (MI)
21. Wisconsin (WI)
22. Michigan (MI)
23. Illinois (IL)
24. Indiana (IN)
25. Ohio (OH)

United States Cities

1. New York, NY
2. Los Angeles, CA
3. Chicago, IL
4. Houston, TX
5. Philadelphia, PA
6. San Diego, CA
7. Detroit, MI
8. Dallas, TX
9. Phoenix, AZ
10. San Antonio, TX
11. San Jose, CA
12. Baltimore, MD
13. Indianapolis, IN
14. San Francisco, CA
15. Jacksonville, FL
16. Columbus, OH
17. Milwaukee, WI
18. Memphis, TN
19. Washington, DC
20. Boston, MA
21. Seattle, WA
22. El Paso, TX
23. Cleveland, OH
24. New Orleans, LA
25. Nashville, TN

Outer Space

1. Mercury
2. Venus
3. Earth
4. Mars
5. Jupiter
6. Saturn
7. Uranus
8. Neptune
9. Pluto
10. planet
11. asteroid
12. comet
13. meteor
14. solar system
15. universe
16. galaxy
17. Milky Way
18. moon
19. constellation
20. astronomy
21. eclipse
22. quasar
23. axis
24. equator
25. star

162

Geography 1	Geography 2	Mathematics	Geometry
1. Pacific Ocean	1. Canada	1. mathematics	1. geometry
2. Atlantic Ocean	2. Mexico	2. arithmetic	2. point
3. Arctic Ocean	3. Panama	3. addition	3. segment
4. Indian Ocean	4. Cuba	4. addend	4. acute angle
5. North America	5. Brazil	5. sum	5. obtuse angle
6. South America	6. Argentina	6. subtraction	6. right angle
7. Europe	7. England	7. minuend	7. intersect
8. Asia	8. Spain	8. subtrahend	8. perpendicular
9. Africa	9. France	9. difference	9. parallel
10. Australia	10. Germany	10. multiplication	10. congruent
11. Antarctica	11. Italy	11. multiplicand	11. triangle
12. Lake Superior	12. Greece	12. multiplier	12. equilateral
13. Lake Michigan	13. Egypt	13. product	13. isosceles
14. Lake Huron	14. Israel	14. division	14. scalene
15. Lake Erie	15. Russia	15. divisor	15. parallelogram
16. Lake Ontario	16. India	16. dividend	16. rectangle
17. Great Salt Lake	17. China	17. quotient	17. square
18. Mediterranean Sea	18. Japan	18. remainder	18. rhombus
19. Caribbean Sea	19. New Zealand	19. fraction	19. trapezoid
20. Bering Sea	20. Korea	20. numerator	20. pi
21. Nile River	21. Rocky Mountains	21. denominator	21. radius
22. Amazon River	22. Appalachians	22. factor	22. diameter
23. Mississippi River	23. Andes	23. decimal	23. circumference
24. Congo River	24. Himalayas	24. equivalent	24. protractor
25. Rio Grande	25. Alps	25. multiple	25. degrees

Bibliography

Anderson, Paul S. and Patrick J. Groff. *Resource Materials for Teachers of Spelling.* 2nd ed. Minneapolis: Burgess Publishing Company, 1968.

Baugh, Albert C. and Thomas Cable. *A History of the English Language.* New York: Prentice-Hall, 1978.

Bryson, Bill. *The Mother Tongue—English and How It Got That Way.* New York: Wm. Morrow & Company, 1990.

Burchfield, Robert. *The English Language.* New York: Oxford University Press, 1985.

Crystal, David. *The English Language.* New York: Viking Penguin, 1991.

Forester, Anne D. "Learning to Spell By Spelling." *Theory Into Practice* 19, 186–193.

Francis, W. Nelson and Henry Kucera. *Frequency Analysis of English Usage: Lexicon and Grammar.* Boston: Houghton Mifflin Company, 1982.

Furness, Edna L. *Spelling for the Millions.* Nashville: Thomas Nelson Inc., 1977.

Howard, Philip. *The State of the Language.* New York: Oxford University Press, 1985.

Johnson, Terry, Kenneth G. Langford and Kerry Quorn. "Characteristics of an Effective Spelling Program." *Language Arts* 58, no. 5 (May 1981): 581–588.

Lederer, Richard. *Crazy English.* New York: Pocket Books, 1989.

Lederer, Richard. *The Miracle of Language.* New York: Simon & Schuster, 1991.

Lewis, Norman. *Correct Spelling Made Easy.* New York: Dell Publishing, 1987.

Lindzey, G., C. Hall and R. Thompson. *Psychology.* New York: Worth Publishers, 1975.

Lizé, Emile and Diana. *"Dear Teacher" A Collection of Parents' Letters to Their Children's Teachers.* Watertown, Massachusetts: Ivory Tower Publishing Company, Inc., 1992.

Lorayne, Harry and Jerry Lucas. *The Memory Book.* New York: Stein and Day, 1974.

Mathews, M. M. *Words: How to Know Them.* New York: Henry Holt and Company, 1956.

McNamee, Laurence F., Ph.D. and Kent Biffle. *A Few Words.* Dallas, Texas: Taylor Publishing Company, 1988.

Mersand, Joseph and Francis Griffith. *Spelling Your Way to Success.* New York: Barron's Educational Series, Inc., 1982.

Slingerland, Beth H. and Carol Murray. *Teacher's Word Lists for Reference.* Rev. ed. Cambridge, Massachusetts: Educators Publishing Service, Inc., 1987.

Sylvester, Robert. "Research on Memory: Major Discoveries, Major Educational Challenges." *Educational Leadership* 42 (April 1985): 69–75.

Templeton, Shane. "Synthesis of Research on the Learning and Teaching of Spelling." *Educational Leadership* 43 (March 1986): 73–78.

Vallins, G. H. *Spelling.* Great Britain: Tonbridge Printers Ltd., 1965.

Wilde, Sandra. "A Proposal for a New Spelling Curriculum." *Elementary School Journal* 90 (January 1990): 275–289.

General Index

Word Index